Great Women on Stage

Great Women on Stage

The Reception of Women Monarchs from Antiquity in Baroque Opera

Edited by
Kerstin Droß-Krüpe

2017

Harrassowitz Verlag

Cover illustration: Pietro Domenico Oliviero, The Royal Theater in Turin, about 1752.
© akg-images

Bibliografische Information der Deutschen Nationalbibliothek
Die Deutsche Nationalbibliothek verzeichnet diese Publikation in der Deutschen Nationalbibliografie; detaillierte bibliografische Daten sind im Internet über http://dnb.dnb.de abrufbar.

Bibliographic information published by the Deutsche Nationalbibliothek
The Deutsche Nationalbibliothek lists this publication in the Deutsche Nationalbibliografie; detailed bibliographic data are available on the Internet at http://dnb.dnb.de.

For further information about our publishing program consult our website http://www.harrassowitz-verlag.de

Printed on permanent/durable paper.
Printing and binding: docupoint, Magdeburg
Printed in Germany

ISSN 1860-1812
ISBN 978-3-447-10784-6

Contents

Acknowledgements

It is a great pleasure to convey my gratitude to the people who contributed in different ways to this volume and whose help and support made this book possible. Neville Morely (Exeter) and Arjan Zuiderhoek (Ghent), who organise the Antiquity network of the European Social Science History Conference (ESSHC), kindly accepted the panel "Ancient Rulers in Baroque Opera" for the 11th ESSHC in Valencia in the spring of 2016, from which this volume derives. In addition, Arjan Zuiderhoek did us the honour of chairing the session and officiating as a discussant. Financial support for the panel and this volume was granted by the Deutscher Akademischer Austauschdienst (DAAD) and Kassel University. The publication of these proceedings would not have been possible without the help of Yvonne Wagner (Salzburg), who adopted the utmost care in proof reading. Virginia Geisel (Marburg) and Michael Yonan (Columbia) gave invaluable comments on the language and time and again helped with the clarity of thoughts. Rebecca Frei (Kassel) assisted in supplying remote literature.

I owe the greatest thanks to the contributors, who eagerly and light-heartedly followed my invitation to join this project, for their enthusiasm and their insightful papers. I would also like to express my gratitude to the audience at ESSHC for lively discussions, an inspiring exchange of ideas and also for raising unexpected and unorthodox questions that provided thought-provoking impulses. This has been a wonderful opportunity to cross academic borders, to strengthen existing friendships and to make new ones.

Marburg/Kassel, December 2016 Kerstin Droß-Krüpe

Great Women on Stage: the Reception of Women Monarchs from Antiquity in Baroque Opera

Kerstin Droß-Krüpe

Most people consider the opera an absolute and timeless embodiment of art: a good opera can be a pleasure for all senses. The opera genre is entirely plurimedial – using different but closely intertwined semantic levels (drama, music, acting), it offers unique possibilities of expression. Despite its display of numerous clichés, bombast, and unrealistic storytelling – time and again, operas enchant their audience, and we only too gladly let ourselves be carried off into their kaleidoscope of exotic, fascinating, albeit completely unrealistic stories. Heroes and opponents, declarations of love and joy, lamentations, disputes, even death are presented by song and music. Different directors, approaches, stage designs, conductors and actors constantly offer new and very own interpretations. They may meet or dash the audiences' expectations, come as a surprise or irritation, opulent or puristic, traditional or highly topical.

So, should opera be seen as an elaborate artistic form, made for music enthusiasts, musicians, and musicologists? The contributors to this volume unanimously consider it more than that: namely, a subject of historical, political and gender-specific analysis. This opinion is recently shared by many others.[1] Although opera had mostly been ignored by science for a long time – which is rather surprising, considering its socio-political relevance –, this imbalance was slowly compensated since the mid 1980s.[2] Musicologists are clearly pioneers in this scientific field; one may mention in particular John Rosselli[3], Jane Fulcher[4] and Anselm Gerhard[5]. Historical science approached the subject only hesitantly; Ute Daniel[6] and James Johnson[7] can be seen as pioneers. They focused on the receptive behaviour of the opera audience, which – in contrast to musicological topics – is relatively often

1 E.g. Ther 2010a: 176; Manuwald 2013; Assmann 2015.

2 Ther 2010b: 9–10. Special mention must be made of the research project "Oper im Wandel der Gesellschaft. Die Musikkultur europäischer Metropolen im langen 19. Jahrhundert" 2005–2009, founded by the Volkswagenstiftung. The project focused on the social and institutional changes, but also on the social phenomena within the unique musical cosmos opera.

3 E.g. Rosselli 1984, 1992 and 1994.

4 Fulcher 1987.

5 E.g. Gerard 1998 and 2000.

6 Daniel 1995.

7 Johnson 1995.

the object of historical studies on opera, since the expectations and reactions of the audience depends on its cultural background and its cultural experience.[8]

In the case of baroque opera, its reception by historical scientists was often biased by large and splendid performances on courtly stages, and interpreted unilaterally as an art form of the ruling class.[9] In fact, the first opera stages were found at the princely houses and royal courts of the 17th century, and they were commissioned by the rulers. This linkage between baroque opera and monarchy remained until the 19th century, at least in cities of residence. Yet soon, the baroque opera also became addressed to the wide public: in the early 17th century, public opera houses opened up[10], and in the course of the late 17th century, an opera business established itself, where the audience – separated by social status – enjoyed performances in return of a – mostly moderate – payment.[11]

This diversification naturally had a significant influence on the content of operas which were presented on royal and public stages, respectively. Whereas on royal stages, an opera was mostly shown only once, the public operas – being financially dependent on entrance fees – aimed to attract the widest possible audience.

As a result, a much larger amount of opera pieces was staged, and successful operas were shown multiple times. The aim was to constantly develop new plots and meet the audiences taste. The much-cited contemporary descriptions of a disinterested and indifferent opera audience (especially towards the recitatives) originate almost exclusively in foreign visitors. Due to poor language skills, they comprehended the actions on stage only with difficulty. In their view, the local audience seemed quite relaxed, probably not concentrating on the opera, but mostly chatting. This erroneous perception might have been enhanced by the fact that foreign visitors almost never attended the premieres, but rather later performances. Hence, the local audience was already familiar with the settings, and, besides listening, enjoyed extensive conversations among seat neighbours. Indifference towards the stage action cannot be assumed – on the contrary, the audience was very much interested in the opera![12]

8 Gier 1998: 34.

9 Wolff 1964: 442.

10 The opening of the Teatro San Cassiano in Venice marks the beginning of public opera houses. It was opened with a staging of *L'Andromeda* by Francesco Manelli and Benedetto Ferrari in 1637..

11 Cf. Gulrich 1993: 201. The audience in the early modern period, whether on the courtly or public stages, was divided architecturally as well as socially in according to the distance from the monarch's or princes' seat. Thus, the social groups kept to themselves, in the opera as well as in everyday life. Cf. Meyer 2012: 644.

12 Strohm 1979: 22.

In contrast to present times, the opera house of the early modern period did not cultivate a repertoire: the baroque opera was, in essence, a 'premiere theatre'.[13] Between the premieres, stages would present acquisitions of other operas – preferentially of recent date – which had been successful elsewhere. They were adapted by exchange, addition or removal of scenes; revivals, on the other hand, were highly unusual.[14] Hence, the choice of operas, their presentation and interpretation, acceptance or refusal by the audience may impressively cast light on the history of culture and mentality.[15]

Corresponding with the zeitgeist[16], the issues of baroque opera were often inspired by antiquity. Initially, mythological material dominated, but historic figures increasingly came into focus, for example in *L'incoronazione di Poppea* by Claudio Monteverdi (libretto by Giovanni Francesco Busenello) which premiered in Venice in 1642. The operas of this time often centred around a ruler being caught in a conflict between love and obligation. In the baroque opera, the decision is always made in favour of duty; love is finally fulfilled, but only under unlikely and often unrealistic circumstances in course of the final scenes. Baroque opera served as a communication platform – for political as well as social representation.[17] In fact, opera can be considered the multi-media event of the 17th and 18th centuries, in its amazing combination of music, artwork and literature. It was a place of moral and as well as of enjoyable edification, of learning the legitimate organizational structures, and also a mirror of social norms and rules.[18]

The present volume is based on a session of the Eleventh European Social Science History conference in Valencia (March 30–April 2, 2016). This session as well as the resulting volume particularly examine the antique female characters in baroque opera. Agnès Garcia Ventura and Marta Ortega Balanza focus on Agrippina the Younger, wife of the Roman Emperor Nero, as adapted and presented in a staging of Georg Friedrich Händel's opera *Agrippina* at the Liceu opera house in Barcelona 2013. They focus on the miscellaneous gender representations of Agrippina from the ancient sources to Händel's opera and its Barcelona staging – a domineering and incestuous woman on the one hand, a caring and loving mother on the other hand. In Valeska Hartmann's contribution Cleopatra VII Philopator, last empress of the Ptolemies, plays the lead. Different from Garcia Ventura and Ortega Balanza she focuses on visual representations or more specifi-

13 Stallknecht 2001: 142.
14 Stallknecht 2001: 142–143.
15 Stachel 2010: 198.
16 Cf. Kerstin Weiand's contribution in this volume.
17 Ther 2010a: 176.
18 Kiupel 2010: 14.

cally the stage designs used in the late 17th and 18th centuries to create an appropriate setting for this powerful and ambivalent (and often highly sexualised) female character. Both case studies are preceded by an essay about the polyvalence of antiquity in early modern Europe by Kerstin Weiand. She pointedly characterises the reception of antiquity during that time period as being both a complex and dynamic process serving a manner of social, cultural and political purposes.

The female monarchs of antiquity analysed in this volume are sliding on a scale between the two extremes of *femme forte* and *femme fragile*. Opera as a genre facilitates an analyses of the perception of women, the models of femininity and gender relations but likewise allows to probe questions associated with the rightfulness and the exercise of female power on a range of different levels.[19] How historical women are presented and interpreted on opera stages is first and foremost mirroring the actual opera's time of origin – and more precisely the time and the socio-cultural environment the libretto originates in.

As mentioned above, baroque opera provides valuable input on the understanding of perception, production and argumentation of gender roles and gender culture. It has to be kept in mind, that the theatre of the early modern period allowed the privilege of questioning traditional female role models – a fact that is also indicated by the corresponding libretti.[20] During the Baroque period, the dominating femininity discourse underwent a qualitative transformation. Hence, for investigation of questions regarding the interpretation, presentation, and reception of female opera characters, especially the late 17th and 18th century should be revised.[21] Around 1700, the *querelle des femmes* and the *femme forte* dominated the discourse.[22] The *querelle des femmes* are, undoubtedly, a phenomenon of the higher classes; often discussed in the salons of the 18th century and included debates about the women's role in society, desirable male and female attributes and the anthropology of the female sex.[23] Both antipoles – *femme forte* and *femme fragile* – existed side by side: the femmes fortes, which were accepted quite positively in this period, are characterized as females who adopted male virtues like strength and activity.[24] A substantial part of the opera audience derived from the same social strata which were discussing these exact questions. The phenomenon of the *querelle des femmes* can be seen as a background for the reception of women; it undoubtedly had influence on the interpretation of female characters on stage, and

19 Herr 2000: 9.
20 Kiupel 2010: 16.
21 Herr 2000: 13.
22 Herr 2000: 17.
23 Cf. Plume 1996: 15–69.
24 Herr 2000: 23–25. A prime example of a *femme fatale* in this context: Elisabeth I, whose regency can be seen as a heyday for the discourse.

on which themes and plots were chosen for presentation. The *querelle des femmes*, arisen from in the salons of upper class women, thus entered the opera stages of Italy, France, and Germany.

The opera genre enables the analysis of the image of women as well as the question of female power and morality on various levels.[25] In case of the depiction of historic female monarchs, the manner in which they are presented always mirrors its own time – that means, the corresponding libretto's time of origin, as the baroque *opera seria* is at its core a theatre play set to music: a *dramma per musica* in tradition of the antique tragedy.

According to text passages from Aristotle and Plato, people from the mid-16th century believed that the whole tragedy, the actor's parts and the choirs, had been sung.[26] The consequence is quite obvious: in the opera, the sung, not only spoken, lyrics are significant.[27] In 1607, Monteverdi declared "l'armonia serva a l'orazione"[28] and advocated for the *seconda practica*. This style has shaped the madrigals and operas by Monteverdi and many of his contemporaries, but was also highly controversial. The lyrics' content and comprehensibility were immensely important. Their elaboration and precision were the basic prerequisite for a congenial expression in the composers work. This fundamental role of the librettist explains his outstanding importance and their high esteem as artists. Libretti were meant to be set to music, but they could also serve as pure text for a spoken drama. Thus, the opera text always originated first; the music had a secondary function. A successful libretto was often utilized by various composers, a fact which led to modifications and adjustments according to the capacities of the respective theatre stage or performing artists.

But where did the librettists get their ideas? Which sources did they use for adaptation of ancient dramas for the opera stage? And, especially for the 17th and 18th centuries, the question arises: what kind of education and training did librettists receive?

In these times, a career in poetry and writing required a humanistic education; until the 19th century, librettists considered the Latin (and Italian) classics authoritative for their own works. Furthermore, librettists even quoted rather remote antique sources. But it remains unclear whether they worked on these sources first-hand, or perhaps used older libretto- or stage play versions as a basis.[29]

25 Ibid.

26 Pöhlmann 1969: 6.

27 Ibid.

28 Scherzi musicali, therein: Dichiarazione della lettera stampata nel Quinto libro de' suoi Madregali (Venedig 1607).

29 Gier 1998: 34.

Numerous libretti from the baroque period feature the construction of the male superiority being threatened by female charms. On the opera stages, the physical and mental superiority of men were persistently brought into question.[30] The female opera characters which are discussed in this volume often walk a fine line between *femme forte* and *femme fragile*. Female rulers were shown quite ambivalently, a phenomenon which can be seen in opera productions from the early modern up to the present time. This is hardly surprising, since in male-dominated cultures, the female element always is a category *in utramque partem*: the exceptional is both admirable and threatening, particularly because it is unclear whether it is a good or evil force. For this ambiguous source of imagination, female sensuality is a central feature, and with that, female sexuality, seductive power, but also vulnerability. The tension between confident/strong and emotional/weak female figures is of particular importance and seems to have fascinated both writers and audience.[31]

Operas, whether in bygone or present times, are always a part of pop-culture. If an opera is not only regarded as timeless tale, but as a mirror of its respective time, it can serve as a fascinating object for scientists in the fields of history, political sciences and gender studies.[32] Especially the libretti are excellent sources for social history and history of ideology or mentality,[33] as they may reflect contemporary images of women and their discourse.[34] For historians, the particular productions of operas offer deep insights into the reception of social matters, gender models, and life circumstances in their particular time.

Bibliography

Assmann 2015 = J. Assmann, Die Zauberflöte. Eine Oper mit zwei Gesichtern, Wien 2015.

Benz 2015 = M. Benz, Semiramis, Zeitschrift für deutsche Philologie 134 (2015), 347–367.

Fulcher 1987 = J. Fulcher, The Nation's Image. French Grand Opera as Politics and Politicized Art, Cambridge 1987.

Fulcher 2007 = J. Fulcher, Romanticism, Technology, and the Masses. Honegger and the Aesthetic Allure of French Fascism, in: J. Brown (ed.), Western Music and Race, Cambridge 2007, 201–215.

Gerhard 1998 = A. Gerhard. The Urbanization of Opera. Music Theater in Paris in the Nineteenth Century, Chicago – London 1998.

Gerhard 2000 = A. Gerhard, Von der politischen Bedeutung der Oper. Politische Untertöne in der französischen und italienischen Oper der ersten Hälfte des 19. Jahrhunderts, Studi pucciniani 2 (2000), 21–36.

---

30 Kiupel 2010: 27.

31 Benz 2015: 348; Kiupel 2010: 28.

32 Ther 2010a: 176.

33 Kiupel 2010: 36.

34 Herr 2000: 22.

Gier 1998 = A. Gier, Das Libretto. Theorie und Geschichte einer musikoliterarischen Gattung, Darmstadt 1998.

Gulrich 1993 = R. Gulrich, Exotismus in der Oper und seine szenische Realisation (1850–1910), Salzburg 1993 (Wort und Musik 17).

Herr 2000 = C. Herr, Medeas Zorn. Eine "starke Frau" in Opern des 17. und 18. Jahrhunderts. Herbolzheim 2000 (Beiträge zur Kultur- und Sozialgeschichte der Musik 2).

Kiupel 2010 = B. Kiupel, Zwischen Krieg, Liebe und Ehe. Studien zur Konstruktion von Geschlecht und Liebe in den Libretti der Hamburger Gänemarkt-Oper (1678–1738), Freiburg 2010.

Manuwald 2013 = G. Manuwald, Nero in opera. Librettos as transformations of ancient sources, Berlin – Boston 2013 (Transformationen der Antike 24).

Meyer 2012 = R. Meyer, Limitierte Aufklärung. Untersuchungen zum bürgerlichen Kulturbewußtsein im ausgehenden 18. und beginnenden 19. Jahrhundert, in: R. Meyer, Schriften zur Theater- und Kulturgeschichte des 18. Jahrhunderts, Wien 2012 (Summa summarum 1), 639–698.

Plume 1996 = C. Plume, Heroinen in der Geschlechterordnung. Weiblichkeitsprojektionen bei Daniel Casper von Lohenstein und die *Querelle des femmes*, Stuttgart et al. 1996 (Ergebnisse der Frauenforschung 42).

Pöhlmann 1969 = E. Pöhlmann, Antikenverständnis und Antikenmißverständnis in der Operntheorie der Florentiner Camerata, Die Musikforschung 22 (1969), 5–13.

Rosselli 1984 = J. Rosselli, The Opera Industry in Italy from Cimarosa to Verdi. The Role of the Impresario, Cambridge 1984.

Rosselli 1992 = J. Rosselli, Singers of Italian Opera. The History of a Profession, Cambridge 1992.

Rosselli 1994 = J. Rosselli, Opera as a Social Event, in: R. Parker (ed.), The Oxford Illustrated Handbook of Opera, Oxford 1994, 304–321.

Stachel 2010 = P. Stachel, Eine "vaterländische" Oper für die Habsburgermonarchie oder eine "jüdische Nationaloper"? Carl Goldmarks Königin von Saba in Wien, in: S. O. Müller (ed.), Die Oper im Wandel der Gesellschaft. Kulturtransfers und Netzwerke des Musiktheaters im modernen Europa, Wien – Köln – Weimar 2010 (Die Gesellschaft der Oper. Musikkultur europäischer Metropolen im 19. und 20. Jahrhundert 5), 197–218.

Stallknecht 2001 = F. A. Stallknecht, Dramenmodell und ideologische Entwicklung der italienischen Oper im frühen Ottocento, Stuttgart et al. 2001.

Strohm 1979 = R. Strohm, Die italienische Oper im 18. Jahrhundert, Wilhelmshaven 1979 (Taschenbücher zur Musikwissenschaft 5).

Ther 2010a = P. Ther, Die Oper als Quelle der Geschichte, in: S. O. Müller (ed.), Die Oper im Wandel der Gesellschaft. Kulturtransfers und Netzwerke des Musiktheaters im modernen Europa, Wien – Köln – Weimar 2010 (Die Gesellschaft der Oper. Musikkultur europäischer Metropolen im 19. und 20. Jahrhundert 5), 175–177.

Ther 2010b = P. Ther, Einleitung. Das Musiktheater als Zugang zu einer Gesellschafts- und Kulturgeschichte Europas, in: S. O. Müller (ed.), Die Oper im Wandel der Gesellschaft. Kulturtransfers und Netzwerke des Musiktheaters im modernen Europa, Wien – Köln – Weimar 2010 (Die Gesellschaft der Oper. Musikkultur europäischer Metropolen im 19. und 20. Jahrhundert 5), 9–24,

Wolff 1964 = H. Chr. Wolff, Das Opernpublikum der Barockzeit, in: H. Heussner (ed.), Festschrift Hans Engel zum siebzigsten Geburtstag, Kassel et al. 1964, 442–452.

The Polyvalence of Antiquity: Remarks on the Reception of Classical Antiquity in Early Modern Europe

Kerstin Weiand

I. Antiquity and early modernity

To this day, antiquity has always formed an important reference in western society. In this sense, the reception of antiquity is a time-transcending phenomenon.[1] According to Manfred Landfester, it can be described as acquiring knowledge of classical Roman or Greek culture within postclassical nations or societies.[2] As such, the reception of antiquity is far from being a modern or early modern characteristic. During the Middle Ages, the reception of antiquity literally boomed at various times. During the so-called Carolingian, Ottonian or Staufian Renaissance, the political elites were fascinated with ancient literature and narratives and they also tried as well to improve the Latin language according to classical standards.[3]

However, early modern Europe experienced a reception of antiquity far exceeding an earlier or later reception, in quality and quantity, as well as in the attitude towards the Classical Age; classical images, narratives and symbols dominated the political, as well as the cultural sphere. This development went back to 14th century Italy, from there spreading over and, from there, spread across Europe during the next two centuries.[4] The humanist protagonists of this process were – in its beginning – mainly Italian intellectuals. These intellectuals distanced themselves from medieval traditions such as Gothic architecture and academic scholasticism and defined themselves by their search for classical knowledge, language and esthetics. While classical texts had been highly appreciated by medieval scholars as well, they had not yet thought of antiquity as an epoch past. In their eyes, the present was immediately connected with classical times as can be seen in the idea of the *translatio imperii*, the transmission of the Roman Empire to the *regnum Francorum* of the Carolingians and their successors. The humanists, by contrast, perceived antiquity as a time definitely past and opposed to later periods of time. They defined antiquity as a culturally unique and out-

1 Niggemann – Ruffing 2013.

2 Landfester 2005: 447.

3 Walther 2010: 3.

4 Helmrath – Muhlack – Walther 2002.

standing period of time; an example of cultural, philosophical, artistic, and literal perfection.[5]

Accordingly, antiquity was no longer was a part of reality, but rather a place of longing. Underlying this process was a new approach to history. In the humanists' view, history did not appear as a lineal chronology to salvation. Rather, history was structured in different ages or epochs fundamentally differing from each other fundamentally in questions of lifestyle and culture.[6] In this regard, the Renaissance did not 'rediscover' antiquity; it rather invented antiquity as a coherent epoch separated from modern times.[7] This revaluation attributed a new status to antiquity: as an unreached and unreachable ideal it became the paragon for a transformation of the present. This revaluation became obvious in the framing of this process as a rebirth of antiquity; as *rinascimento* or *Renaissance*. First used by Nicolas de Clamanges, a student of Petrarch in 1430, this concept soon spread in vernacular languages all over Europe. The idea and concept of *rinascimento* described a certain intellectual attitude and the attempts to approach classical thinking, as well as cultural lifestyle and artistic preferences.[8] In this sense, it differed decisively from earlier receptions of antiquity. The changing attitude towards antiquity became a dominant phenomenon among European elites, both intellectual and political, and it can justifiably be described as a marker of a widespread consciousness of a new time. The common approach to antiquity furthered a shared cultural identity and laid the foundation for the high esteem in which antiquity was held throughout the early modern period. As a cultural code, it developed a normativity which it retained for centuries.

II. The polyvalence of antiquity

The common passion for antiquity suggests a cultural homogeneity. In highly segmented societies, such as early modern ones, however, the reception of antiquity itself was highly heterogeneous.[9] It mirrored social and cultural fragmentations. Not only was it largely an elite phenomenon excluding large parts of the illiterate population, it also referred to various disciplines serving various socio-cultural purposes. The reception of antiquity can be recognized in very distinctive fields of application: the reception of classical languages and rhetoric, of historiography and literature, of material culture and relics, of arts and architecture, and of philosophy and science. According to the social, cultural and professional perspec-

5 Walther 2007: 665–692.

6 For the changing attitude towards history cf. Muhlack 1991.

7 Panofsky 1960: 43–113; Walther 2009: 670–671.

8 Burke 1996: 19–49; Walther 2010; Nauert 1995. Still influential in regard of our view on the Renaissance and its reception of antiquity: Burckhardt 1860, esp. 171–279.

9 Cf. in this regard the essays in Heinen 2011.

tive, a variety of receptions of antiquity can be identified: The painter received a different antiquity than the physician, the architect a different than the philosopher; the statesman a different than the poet.

The heterogeneity of early modern 'antiquities' corresponded with the manifold political, cultural and social contexts of the reception of antiquity. As such, it can be described as polyvalent, as it fitted into different categories and served various functions. Of course, and those, of course, depended on the individual situation. Nonetheless, certain patterns can be identified. In particular, this paper will highlight five categories, namely:

1. Antiquity as a source of legitimation;
2. Antiquity as a means to formulate identities and alterities;
3. Antiquity as a role model;
4. Antiquity as a social code;
5. Antiquity as a learned diversion.

1. Antiquity as a source of legitimation

Due to its high esteem as a paragon, antiquity played an important part in providing political legitimation in Italy.[10] The idea of a rebirth of antiquity was, from its beginning, closely connected with a crisis of legitimation. Since the 14th century, Italian city-states such as Florence, Milan or Genoa had become economically and financially powerful communities. Flourishing trade and a developing banking sector did not only create an enormous amount of wealth, it also deeply affected the political system of those city-states. Instead of feudally legitimated aristocrats, many communities were now ruled by a patrician oligarchic or by military entrepreneurs, the so called *condottieri*. Well-known examples are the Medici family, merchants who became governors and later grand dukes of Florence, or Francesco Sforza, a bastard son and condottiere who became duke of Milan in 1450. The new elites built their power on their wealth as well as their military strength. Nonetheless, neither economic wealth nor military strength provided a proper right to govern. They lacked traditional, generally accepted sources of legitimation such as nobility or customary claims. Hence, the new potentates were under pressure to legitimize their authority. In this situation, the reception of antiquity proved to be an extremely successful way to smooth the acceptance of their power.[11] By drawing on and furthering the high esteem classical history and culture had, they presented themselves as sponsors of classically oriented arts, as well as humanists who were deeply concerned with the reception of classical literature.[12] In this context e.g. Cosimo and Lorenzo de' Medici favored the neo-platonic

10 Walther 2010: 6–7.

11 Burckhardt 1860: 210–224.

12 Walther 1998: 364.

circle of Marsilio Ficino and the reception of classical styles in architecture and arts.[13] Successful mercenary leaders such as Bartolomeo Colleoni (1400–1475) were memorialized by the first life-size bronze equestrian figures since classical times.[14] These statues were modeled after the famous equestrian statue of Marcus Aurelius which itself was now moved into the center of the newly constructed Capitoline square in Rome.[15]

In this context of a permanent legitimation crisis, the reception of antiquity was established as a new language of political legitimation emphasizing the heroic and political virtues of the current rulers. It soon became part of the political vocabulary of the established dynasties as well, providing a universal language of political legitimation. The image of the ideal ruler changed accordingly: the place of the monastic ideal of medieval princes was taken by the ideal of the heroized prince excelling in military strength, as well as in classical education and virtue.

2. Antiquity and the construction of identities and alterities

As we have seen, antiquity was often addressed in moments of change, classifying and describing new, unprecedented situations. This was also the case in constructing and formulating new identities and alterities. In the light of the reformation, as well as political particularization, the unifying idea of one universal Church and one universal Empire became increasingly obsolete. Furthermore, by intensifying global trade networks, expanding missionary work and beginning a colonization process, people in early modern Europe became increasingly aware of non-European, global contexts.[16] Underlying this new awareness were technical, as well as political and cultural, transformations: the improvement of navigation skills e.g. or the threat imposed by an expanding Ottoman Empire furthered the contact with other cultural spaces. Against this backdrop, contemporaries were concerned with defining their own identity against cultures which were perceived as different.

Not surprisingly, the capture of Constantinople by Ottoman forces in 1453 intensified a humanist debate about a shared European identity.[17] In this context, Europe not only became more and more a geographic denomination, but also a cultural, religious and historic unity. Humanists preferably defined this European identity in regard to classical antiquity. In their description, Europe appeared as a culturally shared space separated from a barbaric rest of the world.[18] Most

13 Field 1988: 10–51.

14 Erben 1996: 149–231.

15 Thoenes 1996: 86–99.

16 Bley 2006: 689–702.

17 For the reception of the fall of Constantinople in Europe see Meuthen 1983: 1–35.

18 Mertens 1997: 39–57.

famously, this concept was marked by the humanist Enea Silvio Piccolomini who ascended the papal throne as Pius II in 1458. In his letters as well as his orations against the Turks, he not only referred to the Ottomans as infidel enemies of the Christian faith;[19] he more importantly clearly defined them as enemies of European culture and lifestyle by referring to their historic origin. Up to Piccolomini, the Turks – in Latin Turci – had been identified with Teucri, the descendants of the Homeric Trojans. This interpretation located the Turks within European traditions. They appeared as part of a European classical heritage. After the fall of Constantinople, however, Piccolomini and others determinedly moved the Turks out of this cultural space by claiming that they were not of Trojan, but of Scythian origin:

> "Not Asians by origin are the Turks whom they call Teucri from whom the Romans derive […]: The tribe of the Scythians came from the middle of a Barbarian territory, an impure and disgraceful people, which fornicates in every possible form of sexual intercourse."[20]

By referring to classical authors such as Herodotus, Piccolomini and other humanists located the Turks outside the civilized world, which was the world united by its classical Roman-Greek cultural heritage. By using classical patterns, they depicted the Ottomans as politically and culturally inferior.

Antiquity, therefore, became a central code for constructing identities as well as alterities helping to create the idea of a European identity. Under these circumstances, the reception of antiquity became a means of coping with the contingency which was provoked by fading certainties in a complex world.

3. Antiquity as a role model

Beside legitimation and the creation of identities and alterities, antiquity also provided a general orientation, along with specific guiding principles. In respect of the high esteem in which antiquity was held throughout the early modern era, classical authors provided didactic tuition and instructions.[21] Classical characters became role models for morally correct and virtuous behavior; classical authors were read and interpreted as guidelines for statesmanship, military advisors, and constitutional manuals. The "Facta et dicta memorabilia" – written by Valerius Maxmius during the reign of Tiberius – provided a collection of historical an-

---

19 Helmrath 2000: 79–137.

20 Kaemmerer 2013a: 515–518; cf. the Vienna speech; Kaemmerer 2013b, 495: "*Neque enim, ut plerique arbitrantur, Asiani sunt ab origine Thurci, quos vocant Theucros, ex quibus est Romanorum origo* […]: *Scytharum genus est ex media barbaria profectum* […] *gens immunda et ignominiosa, forniocaria in cunctis stuprorum generibus.*"

21 Niggemann – Ruffing 2013.

ecdotes and portraits, each featuring a certain virtue or vice.[22] In Renaissance Europe, it became a longtime bestseller.[23] Its popularity indicates the widespread interest in classical examples as guides in the vagueness of the present.

Antiquity, however, did not only provide moral examples; it also served as a political think tank. During the rebellion against Spain, the army of the General Estates was fundamentally reformed by revising military tactics, as well as equipment and training. Though the so-called Oranian army reform created a new military system, its masterminds heavily relied on classical authors such as Polybios or Aelianus Tacticus.[24] The reception of antiquity did not focus on the past; it rather provided instructions for the present and the future.

4. Antiquity as a social code

Even though the enthusiasm for classical culture and history was a widespread phenomenon among early modern political, social and intellectual elites, its reception was not a uniform one. In a highly fragmented society, the reception of antiquity also served as a social code providing concepts and practices of social distinction.[25] Even though antiquity was a political language widely accepted and understood, different status groups developed different patterns of dealing with antiquity. Thereby, they developed distinctive codes furthering the integration within a social group and provided patterns to set themselves apart from other social groups. The engagement of aristocracy with antiquity, to name one example, decisively differed from an academic, non-aristocratic engagement.[26] While the latter was largely characterized by a scientifically standardized dealing with classical texts and artifacts, the aristocratic reception emphasized a certain amateurishness. Printed guides and manuals were recommended to young noblemen to show a knowledge and interest in antiquity, but to keep this interest easy and to avoid by all costs an academic pedantry. The familiarity with classical history and culture was a necessary part of true nobility, doing research, however, was attributed to social mediocrity.

As a result, distinct aristocratic patterns of the reception of antiquity developed, most prominently the collection of antiquities.[27] Being extremely rare and expensive, one needed not only financial, but also social capital to bring together a number of impressive originals. A collection of antiques, therefore, proved the high social rank of its owner. One of the most famous collections of antiques

22 A recommendable edition is: Valerius Maximus, Memorable deeds and sayings I, transl. with introduction and commentary by D. Wardle, Oxford 1998.

23 McGrath 2011: 413–414.

24 Hahlweg 1987.

25 Walther 1998: 362

26 Walther 1998: 367–368.

27 Daltrop 1989: 37–58.

up to the present day is the one of Cardinal Scipione Borghese, nephew of Pope Paul V.[28] Parts of this collection are still housed in the Villa Borghese in Rome, originally built by the Cardinal to display his famous collection. In the eyes of the Roman, as well as European nobility, however, the Borghese themselves were *homines novi*. Patricians from Siena by origin, they had moved to the highest social status only by the election of Camillo Borghese as Pope Paul V in 1605. This new status was highly fragile and bound to the life of the Borghese Pope. To establish the new status as nobility, the Borghese family members had to use the pontificate to win titles, as well as to form marriage alliances with European ruling dynasties. The Cardinal Scipione's collection of antiques, for which he spent a good deal of his time, as well as an enormous amount of money, provided another, extremely successful way to underline and retain the newly won social status.

5. Antiquity as a learned diversion

The collection and display of antiques as a social code was closely connected with its role as a learned diversion.[29] Since the 14th century, the ideal of leisure, of *otium*, became famous among social elites.[30] Underlying this process was the reception of the classical concept of a *vita contemplativa* as being complementary to a politically engaged *vita activa*. Accordingly, it not only described time spent apart from one's duties, but also an autonomous contemplation. The contemplative engagement with classical texts and authors was, of course, one of the most reputable diversions during this *otium*. In this regard, the engagement with antiquity as a pastime honored the one who spent his leisure time with it. These forms of leisure often had a semi-public character. When Queen Elizabeth I of England translated classical authors such as Plutarch and Boethius[31], for example, this act of learned she represented herself as a wise ruler.

III. Conclusion

The reception of antiquity in early modern Europe appears to have been a complex and dynamic process serving various social, cultural and political purposes. Due to its polyvalence, the reception of antiquity, or rather plural antiquities, was especially suitable for the courtly representation of power and the powerful on stage and beyond. In this representation of power, one can identify different overlapping functions: political legitimation, as well as the construction of national or political identities, role models and displays of virtue, social distinction, as well

28 Kalveram 1995.

29 Walther 1998: 367.

30 Schirrmeister 2008: 977–979.

31 Pemberton 1899; Elizabeth I, The Metres of Boethius' Consolation of Philosophy (Bradner 1964: 19–45).

as diversion of the courtly elites. Accordingly, the reception of antiquity can serve as a key to a better understanding of fundamental social, cultural and political developments in early modern Europe.

Bibliography

Bley 2006 = H. Bley, Europäische Expansion, in: F. Jaeger (ed.), Enzyklopädie der Neuzeit vol. 3, Stuttgart et al. 2006, 689–702.

Bradner 1964 = L. Bradner (ed.), The Poems of Queen Elizabeth I, Providence 1964.

Burckhardt 1860 = J. Burckhardt, Die Cultur der Renaissance in Italien: ein Versuch, Basel 1860.

Burke 1996 = P. Burke, Die Renaissance, Frankfurt a. M. 1996.

Daltrop 1989 = G. Daltrop, Antikensammlungen und Mäzenatentum um 1600 in Rom, in: H. Beck – S. Schulze (eds.), Antikenrezeption im Hochbarock, Berlin 1989, 37–58.

Erben 1996 = D. Erben, Bartolomeo Colleoni. Die künstlerische Repräsentation eines Condottiere im Quattrocento, Sigmaringen 1996.

Field 1988 = A. Field, The Origins of the Platonic Academy of Florence, Princeton 1988.

Hahlweg 1987 = W. Hahlweg, Die Heeresreform der Oranier und die Antike. Studien zur Geschichte des Kriegswesens der Niederlande, Deutschlands, Frankreichs, Englands, Italiens, Spaniens und der Schweiz vom Jahre 1589 bis zum Dreissigjährigen Kriege, Osnabrück 1987 (Studien zur Militärgeschichte, Militärwissenschaft und Konfliktforschung 35).

Heinen 2011 = U. Heinen (ed.), Welche Antike? Konkurrierende Rezeptionen des Altertums im Barock, 2 vols., Wiesbaden 2011 (Wolfenbütteler Arbeiten zur Barockforschung 47).

Helmrath 2000 = J. Helmrath, Pius II. und die Türken, in: B. Guthmüller – W. Kühlmann (eds.), Europa und die Türken in der Renaissance, Tübingen 2000, 79–137.

Helmrath – Muhlack – Walther 2002 = J. Helmrath – U. Muhlack – G. Walther (eds.), Diffusion des Humanismus. Studien zur nationalen Geschichtsschreibung europäischer Humanisten, Göttingen 2002.

Kaemmerer 2013a = W. Kaemmerer (ed.), Deutsche Reichstagsakten. Ältere Reihe, vol. 19, 2: Deutsche Reichstagsakten unter Kaiser Friedrich III.; Abt. 5, Teil 2. Reichsversammlung zu Frankfurt 1454, München 2013.

Kaemmerer 2013b = W. Kaemmerer (ed.), Deutsche Reichstagsakten unter Kaiser Friedrich III.; Abt. 5, Teil 3. Reichsversammlung zu Wiener Neustadt 1455, München 2013.

Landfester 2005 = M. Landfester, Antikenrezeption, in: F. Jaeger (ed.), Enzyklopädie der Neuzeit vol. 1, Stuttgart et al. 2005, 447–469.

Kalveram 1995 = K. Kalveram, Die Antikensammlung des Kardinals Scipione Borghese, Worms 1995.

McGrath 2011 = E. McGrath, Antike Geschichte, in: U. Fleckner – M. Warnke – H. Ziegler (eds.), Handbuch der politischen Ikonographie vol. 1, München 2011, 413–417.

Mertens 1997 = D. Mertens, 'Europa, id est patria, domus propria, sedes nostra'. Zu Funktionen und Überlieferung lateinischer Türkenreden im 15. Jahrhundert, in: F.-R. Erkens (ed.), Europa und die osmanische Expansion im ausgehenden Mittelalter, Berlin 1997, 39 –57.

Meuthen 1983 = E. Meuthen, Der Fall von Konstantinopel und der lateinische Westen, Historische Zeitschrift 237 (1983), 1–35.

Muhlack 1991 = U. Muhlack, Geschichtswissenschaft im Humanismus und in der Aufklärung, München 1991.

Panofsky 1960 = E. Panofsky, Renaissance and Renascences in Western Art, Copenhagen 1960.

Nauert 1995 = C. G. Nauert, Humanism and the culture of Renaissance Europe, Cambridge 1995.

Niggemann – Ruffing 2013 = U. Niggemann – K. Ruffing, Modell Antike, in: Europäische Geschichte Online (EGO), Leibniz-Institut für Europäische Geschichte (ed.), Mainz 2013-06-04; http://www.ieg-ego.eu/niggemannu-ruffingk-2013-de, URN: urn:nbn:de:0159-2013052206 (accessed August 2016).

Pemberton 1899 = C. Pemberton (ed.), Queen Elizabeth's Englishings of Boethius, De consolatione philosophiae, A.D. 1593: Plutarch, de curiositate [1598]; Horace, De arte poetica (part) A.D. 1598, London 1899.

Schirrmeister 2008 = A. Schirrmeister, Muße, in: F. Jaeger (ed.), Enzyklopädie der Neuzeit vol. 8, Darmstadt 2008, 977–979.

Thoenes 1996 = C. Thoenes, "Sic Romae": Statuenstiftung und Marc Aurel, in: V. v. Fleming (ed.), Ars naturam adiuvans: Festschrift für Matthias Winner, Mainz 1996, 86–99.

Walther 1998 = G. Walther, Adel und Antike. Zur politischen Bedeutung gelehrter Kultur für die Führungselite der Frühen Neuzeit, Historische Zeitschrift 266 (1998), 359–385.

Walther 2007 = G. Walther, Humanismus, in: F. Jaeger (ed.), Enzyklopädie der Neuzeit vol. 5, Stuttgart et al. 2007, 665–692.

Walther 2010 = G. Walther, Renaissance, in: F. Jaeger (ed.), Enzyklopädie der Neuzeit vol. 11, Stuttgart et al. 2010, 1–18.

The Construction of Femininity in Händel's *Agrippina*: from History to Dramatic Opera

Agnès Garcia-Ventura[1] & Marta Ortega Balanza

> When a man aims at the imperial power,
> There is no mean between the heights and the abyss
> Tacitus (quoting Vespasian), Hist. II, 74, 3

In November 2013, a new production of *Agrippina*, an opera in three acts with music by Georg Friedrich Händel (1685–1759), was staged at the Liceu opera house in Barcelona. The performance was directed by David McVicar and the conductor was Harry Bicket. The cast included specialists in this repertoire, such as Sarah Connolly (a magnificent Agrippina, entirely at home in the Baroque style), the versatile Malena Ernman in the role of the Emperor Nero, portrayed as a wimpy cocaine addict, and Danielle De Niese as a beautiful, erotic and seductive Poppaea, together with David Daniels, Franz-Josef Selig, Dominique Visse and Henry Waddington. This modern, well-executed work was a co-production between the Gran Teatre del Liceu, the Théâtre Royal de la Monnaie of Brussels and the Théâtre des Champs Élysées of Paris.[2]

The authors of this paper attended the performance in Barcelona, and were kindly invited by Kerstin Droß-Krüpe to offer an analysis of the figure of Agrippina, the protagonist as presented at the Liceu. As we share an interest in gender perspectives applied to the study of the past, we were keen to analyse the relationship between historical accounts and reinterpretation and decided to pay particular attention to the constructions of femininity (and, by extension, masculinity) that were in vogue at three historical time points:

---

1 Agnès Garcia-Ventura prepared her part of the paper while on a Postdoctoral scholarship awarded by the Beatriu de Pinós programme (modality A), with the support of the Secretariat for Universities and Research of the Ministry of Economy and Knowledge of the Government of Catalonia.

2 For more details on the cast and the production, and for a bilingual (Italian/Spanish) version of the libretto, see the programme published by the Fundación Gran Teatre del Liceu in 2013. On the Barcelona production and for a summary of the plot, see Meléndez-Haddad – Ortega 2013. For a selection of videos showing some scenes of this production, see https://www.youtube.com/playlist?list=PLNFy9SYLAoR8QFD3Nx48gH2w5PrM4chPC [accessed September 2016]. For a list of some recordings of productions and performances of this opera in several European opera houses and theaters, see http://www.prestoclassical.co.uk/w/58436/1 [accessed September 2016].

1) the Roman world, which served as the setting for the opera;
2) the Europe of the 18th century, when the opera was premiered, and
3) the Europe of the 21st century, for a contemporary view.

Our paper is structured in three parts, followed by some concluding remarks. First, we briefly describe the opera itself. Second, starting from an outline of the plot, we aim to show how Roman authors were taken as an inspiration for both the libretto and Händel's music. Third, we present some thoughts about women's roles and the constructions of femininity in 1st-century Rome and 18th- and 21st-century Europe in which these roles have been re-interpreted several times, with different aims in mind.

I. Händel's *Agrippina* in its historical context

Agrippina is an opera in three acts with music by Händel and libretto by Vincenzo Grimani (1655–1710), a cardinal, diplomat, and member of the family that owned the San Giovanni Crisostomo theatre in Venice, where the opera was premiered on 26 December 1709.[3] In Barcelona, however, the opera was not performed until 2013.[4]

Agrippina earned Händel worldwide fame. This is borne out by the account of John Mainwaring (1724–1807), an English theologian and the first biographer of the German composer. In his *Memoirs of the Life of the Late George Frederic Händel*, published in 1760, Mainwaring admiringly noted the success of the opera, which ran for six consecutive weeks after its premiere:[5]

> "… in three weeks he finished his Agrippina, which was performed twenty-seven nights successively; and in a theatre which had been shut up for a long time, notwithstanding there were two other opera-houses open at the same time; at one of which Gasparini presided, as Lotti did at the other. The audience was so enchanted with this performance, that a stranger who should have seen the manner in which they were affected, would have imagined they had all been distracted.
>
> The theatre, at almost every pause, resounded with shouts and acclamations of *viva il caro Sassone*! And other expressions of approbation too extravagant to be mentioned. They were thunderstruck with the grandeur and sublimity

3 For more details on this premiere (including Händel's cast of singers) and other early performances see the overview, with previous references, by Vitali 2009: 11–13. See also Burrows 1994: 36–37. For an analysis of the relationship between Händel's music and Grimani's libretto, with special emphasis on potential discrepancies, see Sawyer 1999. See also Burrows 1994: 56–59 and Ketterer 2009: 61–85.

4 The only precedent dates from 20 December 1897, when the overture was performed at the Teatre Líric by the celebrated cellist Pau Casals (Bonastre i Bertran 2013–2014: 67).

5 Cf. Saunders 1987: 87.

> of his style: for never had they known till then all the powers of harmony and modulation so closely arrayed, and so forcibly combined."[6]

Further testimony to Händel's fame and legacy after his death comes from the words of Ludwig van Beethoven (1770–1827) presumably pronounced on 28 September 1823, during a day spent with Johann Reinhold Schultz.[7] Schultz summarized the episode as follows:

> "In the whole course of our table-talk, there was nothing so interesting as what he said about Händel. I sat close by him, and heard him assert very distinctly, in German, 'Händel is the greatest composer that ever lived'. I cannot describe to you with what pathos, and I am inclined to say, with what sublimity of language, he spoke of the Messiah of this immortal genius. — Everyone of us was moved, when he said, 'I would uncover my head, and kneel down on his tomb!'"[8]

Händel's *Agrippina* is a transitional opera, situated between what was known as the "Venetian" aesthetic (the tragicomic opera of the 18th century) and the "Neapolitan" aesthetic or *estetica metastasiana* which came into fashion in the 1720s.[9] In *Agrippina*, we find a very expressive orchestral sound rich in timbre which offers a high variety of harmony, melody, rhythm and mastery of counterpoint. We also find a rigorous scenic development of stagecraft whose musical dramaturgy develops the themes with simple vocal line recitatives and *da capo* arias; there are also many brief arias that move the action forward and guide the typical Baroque recitatives, flexible *ritornelli* releasing the voices of the instruments, and finally, a large number of scenes and comic characters which are used to build up the opera. So *Agrippina* remains "Venetian" style – even though, as mentioned above, from the aesthetic point of view the work can be considered as timeless.[10]

As far as the opera's historical context is concerned, *Agrippina* was written, composed and premiered at the time of a revival of interest in Greek and Roman

6 Mainwaring, as quoted in Burrows 1994: 36. For the historical context and significance of Mainwaring's work, see Bianconi 1985.

7 The identity of the person who reported these words of Beethoven's has been a matter of controversy among scholars. For a summary of the evidence favouring his identification with a certain Johann Reinhold Schultz, see Tyson 1972. See also Kroll 2007: 30, note 43 for a summary of the scarce information we have about this Schultz.

8 Schultz 1824: 11. This episode, together with other opinions of Beethoven on other preceding composers and musicians, is also reported by Alexander Wheelock Thayer (1817–1897) in the first scholarly biography of Beethoven. See Thayer 1907: 457 and Thayer 1908: 126.

9 Hoxby 2005; Saunders 1987: 89–91.

10 On this compositional period in Händel's career, see Burrows 1994: 42–59 and 382–383.

Antiquity and especially in Imperial Rome.[11] Proof of this is the creation of societies for the study of philology, literature and aesthetics, which were used as raw materials in the creation of a new genre.[12] In other words, Agrippina was the product of its time and context; it can be considered as the successor of works like *L'incoronazione di Poppaea* (Claudio Monteverdi, 1643), *Messalina* (Francesco Maria Piccioli, 1680), *La fortezza al cimento* (Francesco Silvani, 1699), and *Il ripudio d'Ottavia* and *Nerone fatto Cesare* (both by Matteo Noris, 1699, and 1693 respectively). The last of these operas, *Nerone fatto Cesare*, returned to the stage in Florence in 1708, and as Händel was living in the city at the time it is conceivable that he had the opportunity to see it.[13]

But besides this enthusiasm for the study of Classical Antiquity, the librettos of that time show a clear interest in contemporary Europe as well. Indeed, they were also vehicles for topical political comments. Under the guise of a political thriller set in an ancient Rome dominated by corruption and intrigue, Grimani, the author of *Agrippina*'s libretto and a firm opponent of Pope Clement XI, took the chance to mock the autocratic powers that threatened the Venetian Republic at a time when his city was struggling to maintain its neutrality in a politically turbulent environment.[14]

II. From Agrippina the Younger (1st century AD) to Händel's *Agrippina* (18th century AD): history, stories, and music

The libretto of the opera *Agrippina* takes its plot and the main characters from the works of Roman authors, mainly Tacitus (ca. 56–120 AD) and Suetonius (ca. 69–122 AD). The action of the opera begins in 54 AD, when Agrippina intrigues to place her son Nero on the throne (figure 1). In what follows we briefly present the historical background of these two protagonists, as well as the main excerpts of the libretto which express their desires and actions.

Agrippina the Younger (15–59 AD, a soprano in the opera; figure 2),[15] was the daughter of Agrippina the Elder and Germanicus, great granddaughter of

11 Ferri Benedetti 2012; Ketterer 2003 and 2009; McDonald 2001: 9–16. For a list of operas based on the Classics, see McDonald 2001: 243–338.

12 An example is the renowned *Accademia degli Alterati* in Florence (van Veen 2008).

13 Strohm (1985: 122–124) also notes that during the composer's stay in Venice during the Carnival in the same year, 1708, he probably had the chance to meet some of the singers who would appear in his *Agrippina*. On the paradoxical scarcity of sources regarding Händel's time in Italy, as well as some insights into the presence of other foreign musicians in Italian cities in that period, see Talbot 2015, especially 68–73.

14 On the foreign policy of the Venetian Republic at that time see Panciera 2014: 42–49 (with previous references).

15 For a recent overview of Agrippina the Younger as portrayed in the Classical sources, especially in Tacitus, see Gillespie 2014 (with previous references). See also Barrett 1999,

Mark Antony and Octavia, sister of Caligula, and wife (in contravention of "divine law", see below) of her uncle, the Emperor Claudius (figures 3 and 4). Nero (37–68 AD, countertenor in the opera in a role originally intended for a *castrato*) is the son of Agrippina's previous marriage to the rich, cruel, ambitious consul Ahenobarbus, whom she married at the age of 13.

Figure 1: Relief from the Sebasteion at Aphrodisias showing Agrippina crowning Nero in the year 54 AD. Aphrodisias Archaeological Museum, Turkey (http://open.conted.ox.ac.uk/resources/images/nero-and-agrippina, accessed September 2016)

Eck 1993, Lazzeretti 2000 and Torrego Salcedo 2004 for some nuances as well as insights and remarks from diverse primary sources.

Figure 2: Agrippina's bust, from the 50s AD. Landesmuseum Württemberg, Germany (https://commons.wikimedia.org/wiki/File:Agrippina_minor_Stuttgart.jpg, accessed September 2016)

Even during the years Claudius was married to Messalina, Agrippina, already a widow, did her best to secure the future of her son, Nero, by creating alliances with various men. Finally, after Messalina's death and with the aid of her lover, the freedman Pallas, Agrippina persuaded the Emperor Claudius to take her as his wife. To make this marriage possible, Claudius had to obtain a decree from the Senate nullifying the law of incest between uncles and nieces by blood. Once this was achieved, Agrippina's next step was to have Nero adopted by Claudius – something which proved to be decisive for her son's accession to the throne.[16]

16 Tac., Ann. XII 25–26.

Figure 3: Bas-relief showing Agrippina and Claudius. Aphrodisias Archaeological Museum, Turkey (https://www.flickr.com/photos/69716881@N02/15444482746, accessed September 2016)

Figure 4: The so-called "Gemma Claudia". Five layered-onyx showing Claudius and Agrippina the Younger in the left side and, opposite to them, Germanicus and Agrippina the Elder, parents of Agrippina the Younger. Kunsthistorisches Museum, Vienna (Austria) (https://commons.wikimedia.org/wiki/File:Kunsthistorisches_Museum_Vienna_June_2006_033.png, accessed September 2016)

We see, then, that Agrippina's eagerness to be associated with the Empire and with power (in this case through her son's ascension to the throne) is a crucial element in all these stories. This desire is present in the accounts written by Tacitus, Livy and Suetonius,[17] and in Händel's opera, as Agrippina professes to Narcissus as early as the first act:

> "Or fa d'uopo nella man d'Agrippina d'assicurar lo scettro" (act I, scene 5, *recitativo*)

Agrippina's manipulative nature and lack of scruples are highlighted in the aria *L'alma mia fra le tempeste*, where the oboe reinforces her statement of her confidence in her own abilities and in the results of her intrigues:

> "Quanto fa, quanto puote necessità di stato, io stessa, io stessa! Nulla più si trascuri; all'opra, all'opra! Lode ha, chi per regnar inganno adopra." (act I scene 6, *recitativo*)

> "L'alma mia fra le tempeste ritrovar spera il suo porto. Di costanza armato ho il petto, che d'un regno al dolce aspetto le procelle più funeste son oggetti di conforto." (act I, scene 6, *aria*)

And in the aria *Ogni vento ch'al porta lo spinga*, with the authority and majesty that the character requires, Agrippina calls on the Heavens for help in achieving her goals:

> "Pensieri, voi mi tormentate. Ciel, soccorri ai miei disegni! Il mio figlio fa che regni, e voi Numi il secondate!" (act II, scene 13)

From the very beginning of the opera it is clear that the main focus of the plot is Agrippina's ambition, what was also the main focus of the adaptations of Agrippina as a character for the cinema on several occasions from 1910.[18] Along these lines, the scenery of the 2013 performance in Barcelona heightened this idea, with an omnipresent high staircase which seemed to rise up to the sky and was crowned by a throne: a fitting symbol of ambition and lust for power.[19]

As for the music, the opera begins with a Baroque French-style overture (slow-fast-slow), where the slow, solemn *tempo* of the beginning leads into an orchestral power of expansive gestures which was characteristic for this type of opera. With this soundscape in the background, Agrippina comes on stage, a high

---

17 For comment and critical analysis of this feature as reported in the classical sources see, among others, Mañas Núñez 1996–2003: 204–206 and Cid López 2014: 193–196.

18 For an overview, see Pucci 2007.

19 For some pictures of the scenery of the 2013 performance in Barcelona, including one showing the centrality of this staircase, see: http://www.liceubarcelona.cat/en/2013-2014-season/opera/agrippina/images.html [accessed September 2016].

tessitura role that relies on the force of melodic aria *da capo* with the full orchestral language and nuance Händel used to provide emotional expression. Precisely at this moment, at the very beginning of the piece, Agrippina receives the news of Claudius' supposed death in a shipwreck; in the first scene of the first act, she begins to prepare Nero's coronation:

> "Vuoto è il trono del Lazio, e a riempirlo per te suda mia mente" (Agrippina, act I, scene 1, *recitativo*)

> "Con saggio tuo consiglio il trono ascenderò. Men Cesare che figlio, te, madre, adorerò." (Nerone, act I, scene 1, *aria*)

In the same act, Agrippina addresses the powerful people of Rome from the throne. She announces Claudius' death and urges them to proclaim Nero as emperor, with the help of Pallas and Narcissus, who acclaim for the new Caesar. Agrippina's speech is worthy of a head of state:

> "Voi che dall'alta Roma coll'amor col consiglio e colla forza i casi dirigete, a voi qui regno apportatrice infausta di funesta novella. Amici è morto Claudio. L'infido mar, geloso che restasse alla terra un tal tesoro, lo rapì a noi. Di Roma fact è vedovo il soglio. L'autorità, ch'è in voi, scelga un Cesare al trono, ed egli sia giusto, pietoso e pio qual merta Roma e il mio cor desia." (act I, scene 9, *recitativo*)

However, Lesbo (bass in the opera) announces that the general Otho has saved Claudius and that they are about to arrive in Rome. On learning that Claudius is alive, Agrippina cannot help but exclaim:

> "Perfido fato!" (act I, scene 9)

Agrippina's rival is Poppaea (soprano in the opera; figure 5).[20] Tacitus says of Poppaea that "she was a woman possessed of all advantages but a character", though of "honestum animum".[21] Indeed, in the historical account Poppaea appears as no less unscrupulous and ambitious than Agrippina (and this is the image portrayed in films as well, see figure 6); in the opera, also like Agrippina, she deploys her capacity of seduction from the very beginning. In fact, at certain moments in the Barcelona performance Agrippina and Poppaea wear the same

20 For an overview of Poppaea as portrayed by Tacitus, see Mañas Núñez 1996–2013: 206–207.

21 Tac., Ann. XIII 45: "Huic mulieri cuncta alia fuere **praeter honestum animum**" (the emphasis is ours). All excerpts from classical sources quoted follow the Loeb editions.

dress, which helps to highlight both the rivalry and the similarity between the two characters.[22]

Figure 5: Bust of Poppaea. Palazzo Massimo alle Terme (National Roman Museum), Roma (Italy) (https://commons.wikimedia.org/wiki/File:Poppea_Sabina_-_MNR_Palazzo_Massimo.jpg, accessed September 2016)

Figure 6: The actress Patricia Laffan as Poppaea in the film Quo Vadis (1951) (https://en.wikipedia.org/wiki/Patricia_Laffan#/media/File:Patricia_Laffan.jpg, accessed September 2016)

22 For a photo showing this issue of the same dress in some moments of the scenery of the performance in Barcelona, see: http://www.liceubarcelona.cat/en/2013-2014-season/opera/agrippina/images.html [accessed September 2016]

In 1st-century Rome, Poppaea urged Nero to kill Agrippina, persuaded him to divorce Claudia Octavia (and later to send her into exile, and finally to execute her) and finally married the emperor herself.[23] In a further abuse of power she intrigued against Seneca (Nero's preceptor, chosen by Agrippina) and drove him to suicide. Finally, Nero killed Poppaea by kicking her in the stomach while she was pregnant.

But despite all these horrifying events, in the opera Poppaea is depicted as a sweet, innocent young woman in love (in the aria *È un foco*, for instance, she professes her passionate love). Selfless and loyal, the character of Poppaea arouses the sympathy of the audience; her arias have lively rhythms and a dramatic lyricism. Nevertheless, there is capriciousness to her character as well; Poppaea has been interpreted by Wilton Dean and John Merrill Knapp as "the first of Händel's sex-kittens, a deliciously drawn portrait of a girl who lives for sensual pleasure".[24] Poppaea's aria *Vaghe perle* has a striking rhythmic, melodious, and seductive variation.

The character who is in love with Poppaea is Otho, a role for a contralto with bass notes or even a mezzo-soprano countertenor. The historical Otho, of patrician origin, was actually Poppaea's second husband; he divorced her when she began her relationship with Nero. A victim of Poppaea's intrigues, he reigned for only three months in the period of the four Emperors, and was then expelled from Rome; eventually, he committed suicide. Suetonius[25] speaks negatively of both his physical appearance and his character.

In the opera, Otho, who confesses his love for Poppaea to Agrippina, is the noblest and most sensible character in the cast. In his aria *Lusinghiera mia speranza* Otho is glad to have been named successor by Claudius, but declares that for him his love for Poppaea is more important:

> "Lusinghiera mia speranza, l'alma mia non ingannar! Sorte, placida in sembianza, il bel volto non cangiar!" (act I, scene 13, *aria*)

Despite this claim, Agrippina is concerned that Otho is now the heir apparent, as we see in the aria *Tu ben degno sei dell'allor* (act I, scene 10). Regarding the instrumental accompaniment, in this aria Agrippina's anger is expressed through the sevenths of the bass and cello accompaniment and a string *ritornello* made of three parts after the third section, together with a sinuous chromatic line played by the violins designed to express her passion.

---

23 Tac., Ann. XIV 1.

24 Dean – Knapp 1995: 122.

25 Suet., Otho, 12; cf. Suet., Otho, 3: "Why, do you ask, in feigned honour does Otho in banishment languish? With his own wedded wife he had begun an intrigue".

However, Agrippina decides to hide her feelings; although she continues her scheme, she adopts a conciliatory tone. Her new plan begins to take form in the aria *Non ho cor che per amarti* (act I, scene 23). In this scene Agrippina befriends Poppaea, trying to deceive her into thinking that Otho does not love her, but is in fact manipulating her and using her just as a means to attain the throne. In doing so, she hopes to turn Poppaea against Otho, asking Claudius to disinherit him on the grounds of his supposed treachery and hoping that this strategy will disqualify Otho as a successor to the throne.

Also as part of this new plan, in the second act Agrippina instructs Narcissus to kill Pallas and Otho (act II, scene 16). In the historical account it seems that she actually poisoned them herself,[26] in an act described by Tacitus as *muliebris fraus* ("female treachery").[27] Otho was also involved in the plot with Galba to overthrow Nero but later betrayed him, murdering him and proclaiming himself Emperor. After his defeat at the Battle of Bedriacum, Otho committed suicide by plunging a dagger into his chest. Nevertheless, he seems to have shown wisdom in government; he won the loyalty of the army, and indeed some of his soldiers committed suicide with him.[28]

The first act of the opera ends comically, in Poppaea's rooms. By the end of the first act, Agrippina's new plan seems to be quite successful; in the last aria, *Se giunge un dispetto* (act I, scene 24), we see a hurt and resentful Poppaea plotting revenge after the creation of a web of entanglement and misunderstandings, characters who listen while hidden behind the doors, furtive meetings, lies, fights, and reconciliations. We even see Claudius trying to make Poppaea yield to his desire, in an expression of the idea (common then, and unfortunately still common today, or at least until recently) that women hide their sexual 'incontinence' desire behind a false modesty:

26 Tac., Ann. XII 66–67; Cass. Dio, LX, 34, 4; Juv., Sat. V 147; Suet., Claudius, 43–44.

27 The best-known use of this expression in Tacitus refers to the account of the death of Germanicus, defined as the result of *muliebris fraus*: "For a moment the Caesar revived to hope: then his powers flagged, and, with the end near, he addressed his friends at the beside to the following effect: 'If I were dying by the course of nature, I should have a justified grievance against Heaven itself for snatching me from parents, children, and country, by a premature end in the prime of life. Now, cut off as I am by the villainy of Piso and Plancina, I leave my past prayers in the keeping of your breasts: report to my father and brother the agonies that rent me, the treasons that encompassed me, before I finished the most pitiable of lives in the vilest of deaths. If any were ever stirred by the hopes I inspired, by kindred blood - even by envy of me while I lived - they must shed a tear to think that the once happy survivor of so many wars has fallen by female treachery" (Tac., Ann. II 71). On *muliebris fraus,* see Torrego Salcedo 2004: 200, with previous references.

28 Cass. Dio, LXIII 10–14.

> "T'intendo! Donna casta talor vuol per escusa che s'usi la violenza. Al mio voler non ripugnar, cor mio!" (act I, scene 21, *recitativo*)

Jumping now to the end of the opera, in the third act Otho and Poppaea decide to betray Agrippina, telling Claudius that Nero is a traitor who wants to occupy the throne. Nero asks his mother for protection, whereupon the Empress replies that it is she who will obtain the empire for him while he wastes his time on his amorous pursuits:[29]

> "Ah! mal cauto Nerone, all'or ch'io tutti adopro per innalzarti al trono arti ed inganni, tu seguace d'un cieco e folle amor al precipizio corri?" (act III, scene 11)

At the very end of the opera, Claudius brings all the characters together to ask for explanations and try to discover the truth. Agrippina defends herself by saying that she acted for the sake of Rome and of Claudius; Pallas and Narcissus are astonished by her cunning and skill. Next, Agrippina asks Claudius to trust her in the aria *Se vuoi pace* (act III, scene 14), accompanied by music between the minuet and the sarabande. Finally, despite all the difficulties, the opera has a happy ending: Otho and Poppaea proclaim their love, Nero declares his will to reign and Claudius decides to give both Otho and Nero just what they want:

> "Io dei vostri desir volli far prova. […] Cesare fia Neron, tu stringi, Ottone, la tua Poppaea costante!" (act III, scene 15)

This happy ending is a far cry from the actual historical events,[30] but Agrippina's last line does justice to one of the desires that characterize her most powerfully – her ambition to make Nero the new emperor:

> "Or che regna Neron, moro contenta" (act III, scene 15, *recitativo*)

III. The cultural construction of gender roles: 1st century AD Rome, and 18th and 21st century AD Europe

Ancient Roman women were not allowed to take part in public affairs, which were considered as *officia virilia*.[31] In spite of this, we have seen that Agrippina played an active role in politics. To quote Tacitus:[32]

> "It was an innovation, certainly, and one without precedent in ancient custom, that a woman should sit in state before Roman standards: it was the advertisement of her claim to a partnership in the empire which her ancestors had created."

29 Cf. Tac., Ann. XIII 20–21.

30 Cf. Tac., Ann. XII 65 and XIII 14.

31 Livy, XXXIV 2, 11.

32 Tac., Ann. XII 37.

Agrippina attended audiences with foreign authorities as well, demonstrating the supremacy she had over Claudius regarding foreign policy. In doing so, her aim was "to advertise her strength to the provinces also".[33] Tacitus describes her way of exercising power as follows:[34]

> "From this moment it was a changed state, and all things moved at the fiat of a woman —but not a woman who, as Messalina, treated in wantonness the Roman empire as a toy. It was a tight-drawn, almost masculine tyranny: in public, there was austerity and not infrequently arrogance; at home, no trace of unchastity, unless it might contribute to power. A limitless passion for gold had the excuse of being designed to create a bulwark of despotism."

Thus we see that, despite their secondary role in this patriarchal society, Roman women had some room for manoeuvre.[35] Women were well aware of their role in gaining and maintaining their families' prestige, and indeed they worked tirelessly to keep this prestige alive. Women were forced to marry (or forbidden to marry, depending on the circumstances) because of their public roles as wives and/or as mothers of emperors. Especially women of the *gens Iulia* (of whom Agrippina the Elder, mother of "our" Agrippina, originated), were conscious that they directly legitimized both the heritage of the monarchy and the power of the heirs of their *domus*, the *agnati* of the *divus Augustus*.[36]

This situation may be interpreted in the framework of what Judith Butler labeled the "genealogy of gender ontology",[37] a framework characterized by the relationship between the notions of biopower and gender, which, together with genealogy, politicize the historical process of constitution of the feminine and masculine. Indeed, the fact that dynastic succession in the Roman patriarchal society happened through the female line indicates that gender relations and gender identities were shaped within the exercise of political power. The representations of imperial women idealized the features of the *mos maiorum* and the virtues of the Roman matron assimilated, in turn, to the Greco-Roman goddesses. The main aim of this strategy was to spread the image of women as wives and mothers, linked invariably to the family.[38] This idea reinforced the image of women as dynastic successors, something which in the collective imagination served to support the empire's social and territorial cohesion. Thus, some women of the *domus*

33 Tac., Ann. XII 27. Cf. Tac., Ann. XII 37.

34 Tac., Ann. XII 7.

35 Freisenbruch 2010; Gilbert – Chastenet 2007; Hidalgo de la Vega 2012; Posadas 2008.

36 For an overview of offspring and line of descent in the Julio-Claudian dynasty, see Eck 1993: 8–12.

37 Butler 1990: 32.

38 On the political and cultural construction of motherhood in this historical context, see, for instance, Guerra López 2007 and Cid López 2009.

Caesarum moved from being *mater familias* to *mater patriae*, thus paralleling the *pater patriae*, with all the symbolic dimensions that this might entail.

It was in this context that the women of the Julio-Claudian dynasty took advantage of the institution of marriage to place their descendants on the throne. In doing so, thanks to their proximity to the emperor, they obtained the power and authority which they could not achieve directly themselves. This was a source of shame to some of their descendants, as they had to admit that they had ascended the throne thanks to a woman. Considering that this admission made them vulnerable, some of them acted with unusual violence against their mothers and wives.[39] Nero, for instance, tried to kill his mother several times in a series of staged "accidents"[40] – by trying to poison her, by causing ceiling of her bedroom to collapse, or by sinking her boat.[41] Fully aware that Agrippina knew of his involvement in the attempts on her life and would seek revenge, Nero finally sent assassins to kill her. He then announced before the people that Agrippina had committed suicide because her plot to kill him had been uncovered.[42] It goes without saying there was no suicide; Nero had ordered her murder.[43]

Before dying, it seems that Agrippina uttered the famous sentence: "Ventrem feri",[44] fulfilling the prophecy made by the astrologers at Nero's birth. The astrologers had stated that Nero would reign but that he would also kill his mother, to which Agrippina replied: "Let him slay [...] so that he reign".[45] Grimani includes this in libretto:

> "Regni il figlio, mia sola lusinga, sian le stelle in aspetto funeste, senza pena le guarda il pensier."(act II, scene 20)

We see, then, that women like Agrippina had some influence (direct or indirect) in the political arena, although overt intervention on their part was considered inappropriate. To reflect this, in Händel's opera, Agrippina is portrayed as strong,

39 As portrayed, for instance, in Tac., Ann. XIV 3, 1.

40 For some insights into the narration of Agrippina's death, see Cid López 2014: 195–196 and Mambwini Kivuila-Kiaku 2004.

41 Tac., Ann. XIV, 3–9.

42 Suet., Nero 34.

43 Suetonius (Nero 9) states that Nero gave Agrippina a menial funeral. Both Suetonius (Nero 34) and Cassius Dio (LXI, 13, 3) say that Nero felt remorse for the murder of his mother; she appeared to him in dreams and he believed that she would come back for him. See Requena Jiménez 2006. Cf. Eck 1993: 72–76.

44 "The centurion was drawing his sword to make an end, when she proffered her womb to the blow. 'Strike here', she exclaimed, and was dispatched with repeated wounds" (Tac., Ann. XIV 8).

45 "For to her inquiries as to the destiny of Nero the astrologers answered that he would reign, and slay his mother; and 'Let him slay,' she had said, 'so that he reign'" (Tac., Ann. XIV 9).

attractive and ambitious – all features considered as negative when embodied by a woman. To emphasize these traits, in the performance in Barcelona in 2013, Agrippina wore low-cut dresses, high heels and jewelry: indeed, the title of the review of the opera written by Marta Cervera and published in the Catalan newspaper "El Periódico" (16/11/2013) was "Una Agrippina supersexi".[46] The Classical sources reinforce this portrait too: Tacitus, for instance, describes Agrippina as haughty, tyrannical, merciless, dominant, greedy, intelligent, educated, and incestuous.[47]

With all these epithets, Agrippina is presented as a negative female model both for 1st century Rome (her actual historical context) and for 18th-century Europe (the context in which Händel's character was created). This negative model censured emancipated women who challenged the established system, a system that restricted them to the household and kept them in a state of ignorance and submission, and always subject to patriarchal authority.[48] Livy, for example, held that women should refrain from participating in any matter and should remain under the tutelage of their fathers, brothers or husbands.[49]

Figure 7: Placard of the production of Händel's *Agrippina* by the Irish Youth Opera in 2015 (http://www.irishyouthopera.ie/event/agrippina/, accessed September 2016)

46 The same features were highlighted in the production of Händel's *Agrippina* of the Irish Youth Opera, performed during Fall 2015. As an example, see the placard in figure 7. Cf. the images of the production of the production of the same opera by the Northern Ireland Opera, accessible through this link: http://www.niopera.com/past-productions/past-productions-agrippina.php [accessed September 2016].

47 Tac., Ann. XII 59 and 65, and XIII 13–15.

48 Cf. Späth 2000: 129 for the analysis of this matter as portrayed in Tacitus.

49 Livy, XXXIV 2, 11.

In these characterizations it is clear that women's roles depended on the roles of men. Agrippina's mistake, then, was not just to exercise power (something that was improper for a woman) but to act like a man as well, occupying a position for which she was ineligible. Indeed, the vocabulary used by Tacitus to characterize Agrippina emphasized that in the eyes of her contemporaries she was "acting like a man". Tacitus always associates her with the masculine and, more specifically, with the military – an association depicted as negative, as these elements, once again, correspond to the hegemonic masculine identity. To mention just two examples of this symbolic and linguistic association of Agrippina with the military arena, Tacitus[50] describes her as *atrox* and as *dux femina* ("woman leader").[51]
This sort of "world upside down" was perceived as doubly devastating: it damaged both ideal femininity and ideal masculinity. Within this reasoning, the traits that made up ideal femininity were considered as "natural" (i.e., the inability of women to control their impulses, their portrayal as the "weaker sex"), while those that made up ideal masculinity (i.e., the control over women and over their impulses, and control of the *domus* by the aristocratic *pater familias*) were considered as socially constructed, traits that needed to be trained and implemented deliberately by men.[52] Consequently, what both the Roman authors and Händel's opera want to emphasize is not so much Agrippina's errors but the fact that these errors may be unavoidable for women, as they cannot control their impulses and their "nature", and that these errors are not admissible when committed by men. Men, then, must to impose themselves in order to control their women.[53] Indeed, to quote Thomas Späth, in the opera Claudius and Nero are portrayed as "unmännliche Männer"; they fail in their duty of embodying ideal masculinity.[54]

In the opera libretto, as in the writings of Tacitus, Suetonius and Juvenal, the story is told through the careful choice of elements that help the authors to build their male identities. Tacitus, to build up his identity as a politician, as *pater familias* and as a historian, uses different discourses: political, historiographical discourse and gender-related.[55] In Händel's opera these features are present as well: the political and the historiographical discourses are linked to the political situation of early 18th-century Venice, as we have already mentioned, and the gender discourse is linked to the ideals of masculinity and femininity of the European upper classes of that time.

50 Tac., Ann. XII 7, 3.

51 Kaplan 1979; Ginsburg 2006: 112–116 and 131–132.

52 Cf. Späth 2000: 124–126.

53 Ginsburg 2006: 106–107; Cid López 2014: 183.

54 Späth 2000: 131. Cf. Cid López 2014: 181, showing that when these qualities are linked to women the main aim is to highlight their potential negative effects.

55 Späth 2000: 118.

Finally, McVicar's staging in Barcelona includes these different discourses too, although, in this case, we stress that it is the political discourse that takes precedence. Rather than trying to attribute overweening political ambition to a kind of "natural evil" inherent in women, McVicar focuses on its disastrous effects on a group of characters portrayed as alcoholics, cocaine addicts, sex maniacs, and overgrown children with no control over their desires.[56] Interestingly, despite all their flaws, these characters are the ones who hold power and "run the world" (incidentally, a portrait of those who "run the world" very similar to the one offered by Martin Scorsese's film *The Wolf of Wall Street*, also released, perhaps not coincidentally, in 2013).[57] As McVicar explained in his presentation of the staging in Barcelona, his intention was to draw parallels between ancient Rome and the "decadence and frivolity of the boards of large companies, whose policies can alter the global economy".[58]

IV. To conclude: some final thoughts

In this paper we have reflected on how, in Händel's *Agrippina*, certain elements taken from Tacitus and other Roman authors suggest that altering the "natural" order in gender relations, that is to say, the control of politics and control of women by men, leads to disastrous results.

However, is this portrait of an insidious, ambitious and unscrupulous Agrippina a faithful reflection of the flesh-and-blood woman who lived in the 1st century AD? Rosa Cid López notes that while Agrippina is depicted as possessive, domineering and incestuous in the literary accounts of the Roman authors, in sculpture and numismatics she appears as a devoted, chaste and virtuous wife.[59] The literature has an obvious misogynistic streak; but it remains a highly valuable source, as it provides us with a portrait of Agrippina that is not moved by the

56 For a photo of Malena Ernman embodying a cocaine addict Nero, see http://www.liceubarcelona.cat/en/2013-2014-season/opera/agrippina/images.html [accessed September 2016].

57 Despite this coincidence, McVicar affirmed in an interview with Tom Rosenthal, who also suggested some cinematographic parallels to this image, that the choice was not inspired by any source and that it was even hazardous: "Well, it wasn't a conscious irony. That idea came to me two minutes before I first rehearsed the scene. I actually didn't have a clue what I was going to do. I knew what Nero's emotional state of mind was. I knew that we had to push Nero into a very emotional state. I don't know where that idea came from" (http://www.independent.co.uk/arts-entertainment/music/features/handels-agrippina-set-to-grip-london-audiences-435404.html [accessed November 2016]).

58 As quoted in Cervera ("El Periódico", 16/11/2013): "la decadencia y frivolidad de los consejos de administración de las grandes compañías, cuyas políticas pueden alterar la economía mundial". English translation cited in the main text is ours.

59 Cid López 2014: 184. Cf. Ginsburg 2006: 106–132. For her representation in numismatics, see also Eck 1993: 41–42 and 53–59.

interests of the imperial household. Needless to say, the dynasty used sculpture and numismatics as propaganda to highlight the traits of an ideal femininity that were considered positive and desirable.

Cid López[60] also notes that a careful reading of the literary sources provides another possible interpretation of Agrippina – a positive portrayal as a woman who fits the contemporary ideal of motherhood. On this view, she merely followed the tradition of the good matrons, who wanted only to provide their children with the best possible future. If the Roman authors' portrayal of Agrippina is generally negative, this is because, in pursuing this honourable goal, she triggered actions that changed the destiny of the Empire, and her involvement was considered a form of interference in the male arena. Indeed, her actions were perceived as going beyond what was appropriate female behaviour, and were therefore seen as undesirable: hence Tacitus' stories of the evils that may come to pass if political power is left in the hands of women.

Interestingly, this negative portrait of women in power is present in sources from Classical Antiquity and in Händel's *Agrippina*, but far less so in the Barcelona performance of 2013. McVicar seems to attach more importance to portraying the corruption of those in power (regardless of their gender) than to emphasizing the "wickedness" of women. In doing so, he places status and power, not gender, at center stage. Might this be considered as a positive development in comparison to the other sources, as something that leaves behind the misogyny present in the Roman authors and in Händel's opera? Can we assume that this is a sign that times have changed? Or on the contrary, is the idea that women should not be involved in the male domain of politics still present, but is just expressed in more subtle ways, because the open misogyny of the 1st century and 18th century AD sources analyzed here is no longer admissible? McVicar in an interview in 2007[61] pointed out he had interest on highlighting in his production of Händel's *Agrippina*, as well as in his production of another opera with music by Händel, *Giulio Cesare*, "the power of sex", leaving open then the answers to these questions. Indeed, luckily, in our view, these and other questions remain open in McVicar's production, and allow us to reflect on the way gender relationships and power relationships are shaped and portrayed in different historical contexts, including our own.

60 Cid López 2014: 198. Cf. Gillespie 2014: 274–276.

61 See some excerpts of the interview in: http://www.independent.co.uk/arts-entertainment/music/features/handels-agrippina-set-to-grip-london-audiences-435404.html [accessed November 2016].

Bibliography

Barrett 1999 = A. Barrett, Agrippina. Sex, Power, and Politics in the Early Empire, London 1999.

Bianconi 1985 = L. Bianconi, Premessa del curatore, in: L. Bianconi (ed.), John Mainwaring: Memorie della vita del fu G.F. Händel, Torino 1985, 1–16.

Bonastre i Bertran 1994 = F. Bonastre i Bertran, Recepció de la música de Georg Friedrich Händel a la Barcelona del segle XIX, Recerca Musicològica 20-21 (2013–2014), 47–81.

Burrows 1994 = D. Burrows, Handel, Oxford 1994.

Butler 1990 = J. Butler, Gender Trouble. Feminism and the Subversion of Identity, London – New York 1990.

Cervera 2013 = M. Cervera, Una Agrippina supersexi, El Periódico (16/11/2013): http://www.elperiodico.com/es/noticias/ocio-y-cultura/una-agrippina-supersexi-2842799 [accessed August 2016].

Cid López 2009 = R. M. Cid López, Madres para Roma. Las 'castas' matronas y la res publica, in: R. M. Cid López (ed.), Madres y maternidades: construcciones culturales en la civilización clásica, Oviedo 2009, 155–182.

Cid López 2010 = R. M. Cid López, Mujeres 'poderosas' del Imperio romano en la historiografía moderna. Algunas notas críticas a las visiones de la Ilustración y su influencia, in: C. Fornis – J. Gallego – P. M. López Barja (eds.), Dialéctica histórica y compromiso social. Homenaje a Domingo Plácido, Madrid 2010, 685–702.

Cid López 2014 = R. M. Cid López, Imágenes del poder femenino en la Roma antigua. Entre Livia y Agripina, Asparkia 25 (2014), 179–201.

Dean – Knapp 1995 = W. Dean – J. M. Knapp, Handel's operas 1704-1726, Oxford 1995.

Eck 1993 = W. Eck, Agrippina, die Stadtgründerin Kölns, Köln 1993 (Schriftenreihe der Archäologischen Gesellschaft Köln 22).

Ferri Benedetti 2012 = F. Ferri Benedetti, El legado de la tradición clásica. El caso de la ópera barroca, Florentia iliberritana: Revista de estudios de antigüedad clásica 23 (2012), 45–62.

Freisenbruch 2010 = A. Freisenbruch, The First Ladies of Rome, London 2010.

Gilbert – Chastenet 2007 = F. Gilbert – D. Chastenet, La femme romaine au debut de l'Empire, Paris 2007.

Gillespie 2014 = C. Gillespie, Agrippina the Younger: Tacitus' *Unicum Exemplum*, in: J. Ker – C. Pieper (eds.), Valuing the Past in the Graeco-Roman World. Proceedings from the Penn-Leiden Colloquia on Ancient Values VII, Leiden – Boston 2014, 269–293.

Ginsburg 2006 = J. Ginsburg, Representing Agrippina. Constructions of Female Power in the Early Roman Empire, Oxford 2006.

Guerra López 2007 = S. Guerra López, "Hiéreme en el vientre". Poder, violencia y maternidad en la Domus Augusta, in: M. D. Molas Font (ed.), Violencia deliberada. Las raíces de la violencia patriarcal, Barcelona 2007, 151–160.

Hidalgo de la Vega 2012 = M. J. Hidalgo de la Vega, Las emperatrices romanas. Sueños de púrpura y poder oculto, Salamanca 2012.

Hoxby 2005 = B. Hoxby, The Doleful Airs of Euripides: The Origins of Opera and the Spirit of Tragedy Reconsidered, Cambridge Opera Journal 17, 3 (2005), 253–269.

Kaplan 1979 = M. Kaplan, *Agrippina semper atrox*: a Study in Tacitus' Characterization of Women, in: C. Deroux (ed.), Studies in Latin Literature and Roman History 1, Bruxelles 1979 (Collection Latomus 164), 410–417.

Ketterer 2003 = R. C. Ketterer, Why Early Opera is Roman and not Greek, Cambridge Opera Journal 15, 1 (2003), 1–14.

Ketterer 2009 = R. C. Ketterer, Ancient Rome in Early Opera, Urbana 2009.

Kroll 2007 = M. Kroll, Johann Nepomuk Hummel. A Musician's Life and World, Lanham, Maryland – Toronto – Plymouth 2007.

Lazzeretti 2000 = A. Lazzeretti, Riflessioni sull'opera autobiográfica di Agrippina Minore, Studia Historica: Historia Antigua 18 (2000), 177–190.

Liceu 2013 = Fundación Gran Teatre del Liceu, Agrippina, Barcelona 2013.

Mambwini Kivuila-Kiaku 2004 = J. Mambwini Kivuila-Kiaku, Histoire et Rhétorique dans la textualité de la mort d'Agrippine (Tacite, Annales XIV, 1–13), Revista de Estudios Latinos 4 (2004), 87–101.

Mañas Núñez 1996–2003 = M. Mañas Núñez, Mujer y sociedad en la Roma Imperial del siglo I, Norba. Revista de Historia 16 (1996–2003), 191–207.

McDonald 2001 = M. McDonald, Sing Sorrow. Classics, History, and Heroines in Opera, Westport, Connecticut – London 2001 (Contributions to the Study of Music and Dance 62).

Meléndez-Haddad – Ortega Balanza 2013 = P. Meléndez-Haddad – M. Ortega Balanza, Agrippina, culebrón político, Ópera actual 164 (2013), 34–35.

Panciera 2014 = W. Panciera, La Repubblica di Venezia nel Settecento, Roma 2014.

Posadas 2008 = J. L. Posadas, Emperatrices y princesas de Roma, Madrid 2008.

Pucci 2007 = G. Pucci, Agrippina sullo schermo, in: M. Moltesen – M. Nielsen (eds.), Agrippina Minor. Life and Afterlife – Liv og eftermaele, Copenhagen 2007, 161–169.

Requena Jiménez 2006 = M. Requena Jiménez, Nerón y los manes de Agripina, Historiae 3 (2006), 83–108.

Saunders 1987 = H. S. Saunders, Handel's 'Agrippina': The Venetian Perspective, Göttinger Händel-Beiträge III (1987), 87–98.

Rosenthal 2007 = T. Rosenthal, Handel's 'Agrippina' set to grip London audiences, Independent (04/02/2007): http://www.independent.co.uk/arts-entertainment/music/features/handels-agrippina-set-to-grip-london-audiences-435404.html [accessed November 2016].

Sawyer 1999 = J. E. Sawyer, Irony and Borrowing in Handel's 'Agrippina', Music and Letters 80, 4 (1999), 531–559.

Schultz 1824 = J. R. Schultz, A Day with Beethoven. Extract of a Letter from Vienna to a Friend in London, The Harmonicon. A Journal of Music 2 (1824), 10–11.

Späth 2000 = T. Späth, Agrippina minor: Frauenbild als Diskurskonzept, in: C. Kunst – U. Riemer (eds.), Grenzen der Macht. Zur Rolle der römischen Kaiserfrauen, Stuttgart 2000, 116–133.

Stohm 1985 = R. Strohm, I libretti italiani di Händel, in: L. Bianconi (ed.), John Mainwaring: Memorie della vita del fu G.F. Händel, Torino 1985, 117–174.

Talbot 2015 = M. Talbot, Et in Italia ego. Musicians and the Experience of Italy, 1650–1750, in: A.-M. Goulet – G. zur Nieden (eds.), Europäische Musiker in Venedig, Rom und Neapel (1650–1750) / Les Musiciens européens à Venise, Rome et Naples (1650–1750) / Musicisti europei a Venezia, Roma e Napoli (1650–1750), Kassel – Basel – London – New York – Praha 2015, 68–84.

Thayer 1907 = A. W. Thayer, Ludwig van Beethovens Leben (Vierter Band), Leipzig 1907.

Thayer 1908 = A. W. Thayer, Ludwig van Beethovens Leben (Fünfter Band), Leipzig 1908.

Torrego Salcedo 2004 = M. E. Torrego Salcedo, Agripina la Menor, el poder como obsesión, in: J. de la Villa (ed.), Mujeres de la Antigüedad, Madrid 2004, 199–224.

Tyson 1972 = A. Tyson, J. R. Schultz and his Visit to Beethoven, The Musical Times 113 (1972), 450–451.

van Veen 2008 = H. T. van Veen, The Accademia degli Alterati and Civic Virtue, in: A. van Dixhoorn – S. Speakman Sutch (eds.), The Reach of the Republic of Letters. Literary and Learned Societies in Late Medieval and Early Modern Europe, Leiden 2008 (Brill's Studies in Intellectual History 168), 235–308.

Vitali 2009 = C. Vitali, Agrippina, in: A. Landgraf – D. Vickers (eds.), The Cambridge Handel Encyclopedia, Cambridge 2009, 11–13.

Cleopatra in Baroque Opera: the Stage Design Between Depiction of Power and Adoption of Antiquity

Valeska Hartmann

Passion, conflict, betrayal, murder, atonement, requited and unrequited love make the core substance of a baroque libretto. If we add the spice of remote countries, foreign customs, exotic rituals, and a wise or often dubious ruler, we get a cheerful mélange which often defies the laws of historical accuracy – the baroque opera. While up until the 1640s, the dominant figures in an opera's plot were the heroes and gods of Ancient Greek or Roman mythology, the mid-seventeenth century saw an increasing conquest of the opera stage by historical themes. Instead of the gods' stories, the stories of human passion and the conflict between duty and love were told in tales and songs, and presented against the background of magnificent stage designs.

The historical figure of Cleopatra VII Philopator is undoubtedly amongst the most famous and most notorious women in history and was perfectly suited for the dramaturgical scheme of baroque opera librettos. With all the legends and anecdotes of that were spun around her, depicting her decadence, luxury, beauty, magnificence, and the ability to make powerful men succumb to her will, Cleopatra fulfilled all of the fundamental requirements of the genre. In result, she became a character of great glamour and the most depicted figure in opera since the mid seventeenth century.[1] However, the image of Cleopatra created by opera is by no means consistent – it is in fact more ambivalent than one would assume. In the baroque opera, the depiction of her character oscillates between the poles of a power-hungry, lust-driven, hypocritical ruler[2] and an idealised faithful and self-sacrificing lover.[3] These at times complex and multi-facetted conceptions of character show the librettos' interaction with their literary models, which from

1 Cleopatra is the subject of numerous opera libretti, ranging from the baroque up until the modern period. For lists of Cleopatra depictions, see Reischert 2001, 578–584; Stieger 1975: 252.

2 See *Die betrogene Staats-Liebe /oder/ Die unglückliche Cleopatra, Königin von Ägypten* (Music: Johann Mattheson, Libretto: Friedrich Christian Feustking, premiere: 20 October 1704, Theater am Gänsemarkt, Hamburg), in which Cleopatra is reduced to the role of the lustful seductress.

3 See *Giulio Cesare in Egitto* (Music: Georg Friedrich Händel, Libretto: Nicola Francesco Haym, premiere: 2 March 1724, King's Theatre Haymarket, London), in which Cleopatra is depicted as a *femme fatale* with political savvy; however her intentions seem legitimate at the outset. Her initial coquetry finally turns into true and deep love.

antiquity, through the Middle Ages, and up until the Renaissance created varying images of Cleopatra.[4] While the Augustan victors' historiography reduced Cleopatra to the double role of the seductress of Marc Antony and the external enemy of Rome[5], medieval depictions tend to be more heterogenous. Reference to her person mostly served as a depiction of moral transgression, in particular lust and ostentation, employing the moral principle of the negative example.[6] In the Renaissance, the list of themes is extended to include such traits as decadence, immodesty, as well as a lack of chastity and virtue in Francesco Petrarca's writings.[7] These were the themes on which the authors in the seventeenth century could rely and which they could further develop. It is thus hardly surprising that in baroque literature, Cleopatra first became the embodiment of the demonic shrew worshipped by men, who were most often represented in the figure of a feeble Marc Antony.[8] However, along with the role of the hypocritical trickster[9], the depiction of Cleopatra as a faithful and self-sacrificing lover increasingly gained in popularity.[10] Concentration on the actual love story led authors to eliminate any political elements and thus favour the depiction of a genuine love tragedy. This practice was adopted by librettists of the baroque opera as they moved Cleopatra's political narrative more and more into the background to allow more space for a flamboyant love tale.

The observation that librettos of operas with historical themes are an important medium of accessing information about historical figures was most recently made by Gesine Manuwald in her 2013 book, *Nero in Opera. Librettos as*

4 On the development of the Cleopatra image in antique Augustaen historiography up until the Renaissance, see Feichtinger 1996: 89–111; Frenzel 2005: 509–514; Simonis 2004, 273–292; Marquardt 2013: 553.

5 Propertius refers to Cleopatra as a whorring Queen (3, 11, 39); Lucan calls her a disgrace to Egypt, a abominable harpy whose lust takes a heavy toll on Rome (10, 53–69); Pliny the Elder emphasised her wastefulness, arrogance, and extravagance (NH 9, 119–121); Plutarch stresses her attractiveness to Marc Antony (Antony 90); in Horace (carm. 1, 37), she is referred to as a horrid demon of doom, as a fatal monstrum in league with a rabble of deranged men.

6 Depictions of Cleopatra as a lustful woman in: Dante Alighieri, Divina Commedia, Inf. 5, 63.

7 Francesco Petrarca, Trionfi della Forma 2, 106–107 and 1, 22–26; also Giovanni Boccaccio, De Claris Mulieribus 38, 140–141, who has presented Cleopatra as the negative character of a *femme fatale* who is conscious of her power and with her beauty entangles men in amorous dependence with.

8 Hans Sachs, Die Königin Cleopatra mit Antonio dem Römer, 1560; moralising judgment condemning the arrogance, lust, and unfaithfulness.

9 Charles Sedley, Antony and Cleopatra, 1677; Daniel Caspar von Lohenstein, Cleopatra, 1677.

10 Thomas May, The Tragedy of Cleopatra, Queen of Egypt, 1626; John Dryden, All for Love, 1678.

Transformations of Ancient Sources. The present essay will be probed the question up to what extent her described historical transformation processes of ancient sources can also be observed in the stage design of the baroque opera, whether the plot and stage design follow the ancient space described by libretto. The essay is a first introduction to the topic using the remaining concepts of the stage designs for the opera *Cleopatra* from 1690. The question of whether stage designs were even meant to evoke historical and geographical truth, to me, is crucial for shedding further light on the specific functions of stage designs in the baroque opera. To this end, a preliminary discussion and reconstruction of the available sources of Egypt as a historical setting would be reasonable. It can be observed that frequently not the accessibility of sources alone determined the visual representation in the adoption of the ancient content, but that political and social factors also played a central role. The ways in which the stage design could deviate from the libretto is another pointer to the role it may have played in the larger artwork of the opera.[11] In order to illustrate the transformative power of this function, the concepts of the stage design for *Cleopatra* (1690, Braunschweig, Hagenmarkt) are compared to the stage design of *La morte di Cleopatra* (1797, Bologna, Teatro Comunale di Bologna), which in its visual message already transports a completely different idea of Ancient Egypt.

I. The scene-painter Johann Oswald Harms and his depiction of Egypt in *Cleopatra* (1690)

The opera, *Cleopatra*, consisting of an overture[12] and three acts, premiered at the opening ceremony for the new opera Braunschweig Hagenmarkt.[13] The libretto was written by the famous baroque court poet Friedrich Christian Bressand (1670–1699) and was put to music by Johann Sigismund Kusser (1660–1727). The stage designs, whose concept sketches have survived, were created by Johann Oswald Harms (1643–1708), one of the key representatives of decorative monu-

11 In opera, a combination of different art forms is at work. Music and libretto are complemented by a stage design. This does not only include the painted scene, but also the elements of lighting, costumes, and stage props.

12 The overture preceding the actual opera had no thematic connection with the ancient story's content; it only served as praise for the attending Princes of the castles Celles, Hannover, and Wolfenbüttel. On the political significance of the overture see Schröder 1998: 24–28. On the presence of rulers and the political significance of the Braunschweig opera see Seebald 2009: 52–53.

13 The date of the premiere has been the subject of extensive discussion. 1690 has become the consensus as regards the year of the premiere. See Degen 1935: 5–9; Richter 1963: 95; Eisinger 1990: 41.

ment painting in the baroque period in central and northern Germany. He is one of the most significant stage designers of the baroque of northern Germany.[14]

The libretto of this opera tells the intricate love story of Cleopatra and Gaius Julius Caesar, which has to – and in fact does – survive in a web of intrigues, false accusations, and feigned pledges of love. Against the historical background of the civil war of 48 BC, the plot is set at the time of Caesar's stay in Alexandria. Following the victory over Pompey, his political adversary, he is received by the Egyptians with great cheer. Assuming it would be Caesar's wish, Ptolemy, Cleopatra's brother, has Pompey decapitated and arranges for the severed head to be handed to Caesar as a trophy – an act of cruelty which Caesar rejects with indignation, but which confirms Ptolemy and Cleopatra as Kings of Egypt.

The remaining parts of the story are pure fiction in regard to the intricacies of their love story plot. While the love between Cleopatra and Caesar is a mutual one, Marc Antony is rejected by Cleopatra. However, Caesar, taking Marc Antony's advice, pursues a hidden agenda and with feigned confessions of love attempts to gain the favour of Cornelia, the widow left by his murdered political opponent, to advance his political strategy. Marc Antony's intrigue becomes more significant as he cleverly manages to let Cleopatra overhear the scene of Caesar's love speech, which she takes as genuine and thus feels abandoned by Caesar and turns away from him in dismay.[15] Furthermore, Ptolemy, Cleopatra's brother and adversary, who is in love with Pompey's widow, attempts to gain her favour with the help of Photinus, his eunuch confidant, in order to form an allegiance with her against Caesar, and thus also against Cleopatra – however, he fails. Meanwhile, Arsinoe, Cleopatra's sister, incites the people against the Roman rulers hoping to climb the throne of Egypt together with her brother Ptolemy. Marc Antony, too, becomes an ally in this Egyptian plot. After the abduction of Cornelia and Cleopatra by their adversaries, Caesar rides to battle as a Roman Emperor and upon his victory frees the two women. Ptolemy falls on the battlefield, his allies are executed, Arsinoe is forgiven and married to Mithridates, the ruler of Pontus; Cornelia is made aware of the falsity of the love pledge she received, Marc Antony is also forgiven; finally, Cleopatra is made the sole ruler of Egypt. The plot is obviously an intricate baroque Gordian knot which only in the end is undone to the joy of (almost) all, thus satisfying the baroque need for a happy ending which sees the triumph of true loyalty and virtue.

14 In Rome, Harms was influenced by the ruin and landscape painters from the circle around Salvator Rose; this is visible in all his later design drafts, particularly in the ruin pictures. On the biography see Tintelnot 1939: 62; Stolberg-Wernigerode 1966: 684–685.

15 In typical baroque manner, Cleopatra's aria has her bemoan the fate of kings: a dim picture of the ruler's duties and the dark parts of their existence, expressing the topos of royal melancholy. See Eisinger 1990: 46–47.

Unlike the intricacies of the love story plot, which, as mentioned above, were pure fiction, the political events and the acting figures in them seem to be largely based on historical facts. The only remaining libretto of a 1691 reproduction of the opera does not feature an *argomento* with possible referenced sources. Instead of this otherwise typical list of source references, which serves not only to evoke historical accuracy, but also to attest to the librettist's erudition, we find an elaborate and submissive dedication to Duke Ludwig Rudolf of Braunschweig Wolfenbüttel and his wife Duchess Christine Luise of Oettingen-Oettingen prefacing the story, revealing the representative character of the production.[16] Whether the original libretto from 1690 was prefaced with an *argomento*, can so far not be ascertained.

The total of remaining design drawings, aside from those for the overture,[17] consists of the sketches, albeit incomplete, for three scenes of *Cleopatra*. Two scenes in the remaining drafts show designs which I will discuss in this essay.[18] They are both grey pen drawings on paper washed with grey ink showing the respective settings in Alexandria. The design for act II, scene 8, in the two remaining right sceneries shows a royal palace in Alexandria (figure 1).[19] The specific architecture is that of a palace with columns of the Corinthian order. The front pair of pillars marks the entrance to a pillar hall lying beyond. This entrance function is shown by the fluted pillars which at the bottom feature additional twisted flutings resting on ornamented column pedestals. In the adjacent building part, there are also Corinthian-order columns, whose surface, however, is clearly smooth, and whose bottom part, although also fluted, is not twisted. Between the pillars,

16 The representative character is also visible in the mere wording found on the title page: "Cleopatra/ Sing Spiel/ Auf dem grossen Braunschweigischen/ Schauplatz/ vorzustellen/ im Jahr 1691./ Dem/ Durchleuchtigen Prinzen/ Herrn/ Ludwig Rudolfen/ Hertzogen zu Braunschweig/ und Lüneburg/ wie auch/ der gleichfalls/ Durchleuchtigen Prinzessin/ Frauen/ Christinen Louisen/ Vermählter Hertzogin zu Braunschw. Lüneb./ gebohrner Fürstin zu Oettingen/ unterthänigst gewidmet von Friedrich Christian Bressand/ Wolfenbüttel/ gedruckt bey Caspar Johann Bißmarck".

17 The stage designs for the first scene of the overture show vedute of the cities of Celle, Hanover, Wolfenbüttel, and Braunschweig as a tribute to the attending dukes. The designs for the second scene of the overture, on the backdrop as well as the left and right scenery, show a section of a contemporary market. The stage directions are: "Der Schauplatz verändert sich/ und stellet einen offentlichen Markt/ ziehlend auf die Braunschweiger Messe/ mit vielen Kaufläden und Kram Buden". Printed in: Stadt Braunschweig 1990: 561–563, cat. no. III. 200–203, 207, 209.

18 The design for a tent encampment, which remains in seven left and right sceneries, for act III, scene 12 is not part of this analysis. The libretto refers to the scene with the words "Der Schauplatz stellet vor das Egyptische Feldlager vor der Stadt Alexandria". Printed in: Stadt Braunschweig 1990: 580–581, cat. no. III. 249–250.

19 Scene description in the libretto: "Der Schau-Platz stellet vor den inneren königlichen Pallast".

at the transversal section, there are two statues of female figures, both lifting their gowns to just above their left knee. The construction is crowned by protruding entabulature and built-on cartouches, vases, and festoons.

Figure 1: Johann Oswald Harms (1643–1708), stage design for *Cleopatra* by Johann Sigismund Kusser, Braunschweig Hagenmarkt, 1690: A royal palace in Alexandria (act II, scene 8) – Two sets of scenery for stage right (1689); grey pen drawings on paper washed with grey ink; dividing lines in red ink, 314 x 156 mm; © Herzog Anton Ulrich-Museum Braunschweig, Kunstmuseum des Landes Niedersachsen

As it is visible in the libretto, the scene is set in Alexandria. However, the use of form and shape in this architecture is not even remotely Egyptian, but fully in accordance with the baroque symbolic tradition. It is therefore impossible for the viewer to place the scene in Alexandria purely based on the visual elements. Cleopatra's palace here appears as a contemporary baroque, Western European piece of magnificent royal architecture and thus mirrors the courtly reality of the current times.

The only remaining complete design, the three sheets for act III, scene 1, also does not allow identification of Alexandria as the setting (figures 2–4). The libretto speaks of a "remote and deserted place outside the city of Alexandria". Harms applied this description by creating a romantic representation of a ruin, which in full accordance with the late-baroque taste shows a poetic and atmospheric scene. The architecture seems Roman, lacking any borrowed content from Egyptian design; the backdrop shows a deserted palace architecture overgrown with vegetation. Behind a transverse pedestal of half-covered arches and traces of columns, a ruin architecture is standing, consisting of dilapidated floors, corridors, colonnades. The left and right sceneries[20] show a debris-covered court framed by irregular ruin parts and several floors of destroyed wall. The ruin architecture is laced and in places overgrown with vegetation. Reconstructing the architecture before the mental eye is hardly possible because the floor heights of the individual components differ from one another. They seem more like individual architectural set pieces of a ruin structure assembled one by one.

Just as in the design of Cleopatra's palace discussed above, this sketch shows no indication of Egyptian-style use of form and shape. Despite the libretto's explicit reference, there is no visible attempt at visually imagining the historical place. Instead, what was created here is a ruin and architectural phantasy that is typical of the late baroque period. The inherent symbolism of late-baroque ruin depictions as an omnipresent *vanitas* symbol determines the overall aesthetic impression of this landscape scene.[21] As the symbol of decay, the ruin is, on the one hand, a melancholic atmospheric instrument showing the grandeur of past times, now in devastation and, on the other hand, a moral warning against the arrogance of man. Locating the plot as a whole in a visually identifiable Egyptian antiquity was not the aim. Instead, the stage design, especially with regard to the visualisation of Cleopatra's palace, seems to correspond with the baroque present, which reveals the antagonism in setting between the stage design and the libretto. Stage design is always a communicative element which functions in direct correlation with the other constituents of the opera.

---

20 To each side, five sceneries were planned and squared for set painting.

21 On the relationship between landscape painting and ruin depictions in baroque painting see Sigmund 2002: 39–40, 51–52.

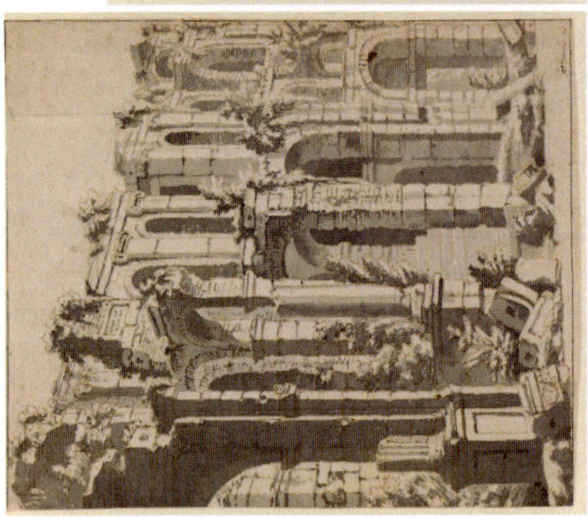

Figures 2–4:
Johann Oswald Harms (1643–1708), stage design for *Cleopatra*
by Johann Sigismund Kusser, Braunschweig Hagenmarkt,
Ruins (act III, scene 1) – Five sets of scenery for stage left (337 × 279 mm),
backdrop (340 × 386 mm), stage right (338 × 287 mm),
grey pen drawings on paper washed with grey ink, dividing lines in red ink (all 1689);
© Herzog Anton Ulrich-Museum Braunschweig,
Kunstmuseum des Landes Niedersachsen

1. The image of Egypt in the 17th century as a basis of reception for the scene painters

This obvious opting-out of a depiction of antiquity in the stage design of *Cleopatra* (1690) raises the question of the specific image of Ancient Egypt at the end of the seventeenth century which could have served as the basis of Harms' reception of this historic age.

Continuing from Early Modernity, which, thanks to Christofor Buonadelmente's rediscovery of the pseudo-Egyptian *Corpus Hermeticum*[22], stylised Egypt as a treasure cove of wisdom as early as 1419, the baroque period is initially characterised by the re-erection of Egyptian obelisks in Rome.[23] Along with this interest in obelisks came an examination of the Egyptian hieroglyphs. The most prominent pieces of this research are the studies by Athanasius Kircher,[24] which mark the intellectual climax of hieroglyph mysticism in the baroque period.[25] Moreover, Jacques-Benigne Bossuet, the tutor to the French Dauphin, in his 1681 work *Discour sur l'Histoire* referred to Egypt as the ideal of an absolutist aetas-aurea.[26] Finally, the large number of travel writings, many of them illustrated, also offered the possibility of acquiring knowledge about the culture and the art of Ancient Egypt. One example is Pietro della Valle who, between 1650 and 1658, published travel letters of his eleven-year journey to the Orient,[27] which also took him to Egypt. By the end of the seventeenth century, various translations of his accounts had spread all across Europe.[28] In other words, the overall situation of available publications would have allowed, at least at bottom, literary and visual access to Egyptian set pieces such as pyramids and obelisks. It can therefore not be a lack of models that accounts for the missing adoption of antiquity in the stage designs. This absence, which can be found also in other stage designs from this period written for operas with historical themes, is owed, instead, to the baroque conception of history, which also includes the opera as an *instrumenti regni*.

22 A synthesis of various writings from Late Antiquity, which were purposely dated to an earlier time and were meant to serve as theological and philosophical edification. 1463 translated from the Greek by the Florentine philosopher Marsiglio Ficino, and printed in Italian in 1471; see Syndram 1990: 22.

23 After 1587, Pope Sixtus V had Rome's obelisks re-erected.

24 Publications: Prodomus Coptus sive Aegyptiacus (1636), Lingua Aegyptiaca restituta (1643), Oedipus Aegyptiacus (1652), Obelisci Aegyttiani (1666), Sphinx mystagoga (1676); also see Curran 2009: 161–178; Leospo 1989, 56–71.

25 On this aspect of Early Modernity see Syndram 1990: 22–23.

26 Egyptian early history and ist architectural and cultural achievements as a model for the absolutist form of government; see Syndram 2001: 1199; Syndram 1990: 23–24.

27 Pietro della Valle, Viaggi di Pietro della Valle il pellegrino con minuto ragguaglio di tutte le cose notabili osservate in essi: descritti da lui medesimo in 54 lettere familiari ... all'erudito ... Mario Schipano; divisi in tre parti, cioe la Turchia, la Persia e l'India ... Vit. Mascardi, Roma 1650–1658.

28 See Hofstetter (2005: 9, 12–13) who also mentions additional travel writings.

2. The conception of history and the function of opera in Baroque

To approach the question of the evocation of historical accuracy in the baroque stage design, we must first address the question, what kind of function the stage design of the baroque opera had. As demonstrated by the German art historian Hans Tintelnot in his 1939 book on the baroque theatre, the seventeenth century was largely dominated by the opera, whose magnificence allowed it to make its way into European royal courts. Without the opera, the ceremonious presentation of the state and the joyous festivities of the baroque period would have been unimaginable.[29] As numerous individual studies show, they served Europe's absolutist courts as vehicles of political messages.[30] The opera as a larger piece of art consisting of the libretto, the music, and the stage design was the period's paramount form of representation of power.

Aside from this political function, another aspect which is crucial to an examination of the adoption of antiquity in the stage design of *Cleopatra* (1690) is the general conception of history in late seventeenth and eighteenth centuries in the German-speaking part of Europe.[31] The image of history in the seventeenth century is in essence still determined by the medieval doctrine of the transfer of the Empires of world history (*translatio imperii*), although there are beginnings of more refined historical thinking in the question of the evaluation and the use of history.[32] Each historical event is comprehended as an *exemplum* or a type, which has a correlate in the present. The historical examples serve as an experiential basis and as proof of accuracy of the transcendent universal doctrines inherent in a given value system. As a consequence, historical figures featuring in operas could be positive or negative mirror images of contemporary rulers. History, that is, served as moral instruction by example.[33] It was this type of thinking in analogies which conditioned the flexibility of the historical concept of plausibility. The possibility of an Egyptian ruler in a contemporary flamboyant baroque costume is nothing but a logical consequence.

29 "Dem barocken Kunstwollen entspricht die in der Oper mögliche Synthese von bildender Kunst und Dichtung. Allegorik und Repräsentation, von Symbolismus und dynastischer Idee war so recht geeignet, den Willen zur totalen Durchdringung aller höfisch-zeremoniellen Bereiche mit dem höfisch-künstlerischen zu verwirklichen. Die Ideen groß angelegter monarchischer Festprogramme konnten in einer Oper Gestalt annehmen, deren literarisch, mythologischer Grundgedanke Bezug auf den festlichen Anlass nahm", Tintelnot 1939: 53–54.

30 See exemplary Rosand 1991; Schröder 1998; Werr 2010.

31 On the conception of history in the early baroque opera and the problem of representation of the aristocracy, see Schröder 1998: 71–81.

32 On the biblical justification of the medieval and post-medieval conception of history and the doctrine of the four monarchies as well as the translatio principle, see Vosskamp 1967: 17–36.

33 See Vosskamp 1967: 38, 43–44; Schröder 1998: 72–73.

The example of the 1690 opera *Cleopatra* discussed above illustrates the depiction of the ruler in the figures of Julius Caesar and Cleopatra, which become the moral counterparts of Prince Ludwig Rudolf and his wife Christine Louise Duchess of Braunschweig and Lüneburg. Caesar's characterisation as possessing wisdom and foresight is accompanied by a faithful, honorable, and strikingly virtuous Cleopatra. Such motifs as hypocrisy, lust for power, or voluptuousness are strictly avoided. What is remarkable about this characterisation of the figure of Cleopatra is that proto-Renaissance, with its most famous writers Dante Alighieri, Francesco Petrarca, and Giovanni Boccaccio, had left for the baroque period a catalogue of motifs for the character of Cleopatra which ranged across such traits as lust,[34] decadence, lack of chastity and virtue,[35] and even a self-confident *femme fatal*-type of character.[36] Now, however, Cleopatra is the faithful lover by Caesar's side, and their true love triumphs over unfaithfulness, betrayal, and abduction by others. It is thanks to the benevolence of the ruler Caesar, that all the intrigues and intricacies finally give way to a cheerful restoration of order. The ending has them both attain their legitimate and divenely-ordained power position – a truly fitting model of a ruler for an opera produced to honour a wedding.[37]

Thinking in analogies is also the determining factor behind the apparent genericism of the stage design in its baroque form variant. The principle of generic types plays a role not only for the visual effect, i.e. the conceptual form of the stage designs, but also for their pragmatic use. For cost-saving reasons, the same stage designs were often used in different pieces, which was only possible because of the highly generic representation of the setting. The topical principle of opera scenes, each implying a specific plot, was summarised at the end of the seventeenth century by Claude-François Ménestrier in his work *Des représentations en musique anciennes et modernes* (1681), in which he identified a total of eleven main decorations (basic types).[38] The librettists knew how to follow these decorational instructions because, with the particular settings, they could be certain that the audience would be familiar with the implied atmosphere and therefore understood it – not on a representational, but on a symbolic level.[39] The stage

34 Dante, Commedia, Inf. 5, 63.

35 Petrarca, Trionfi della Fama 2, 105–106; 1, 22–26.

36 Boccaccio, De claris mulieribus 38, 140–141.

37 "Bressands Libretto erfüllt die Forderungen der barocken Dramaturgie nach einer intrikaten, affektenreichen Handlung, in der sich die Gegenwart in der antiken Handlung, in der Staats- und Liebesaffären eins sind, wiederfindet." (Eisinger 1990: 47).

38 The categories identified by Ménestier are: 1. Les Celestes, 2. Les Sacrées, 3. Les Militaires, 4. Les Rustiques, 5. Les Maritimes, 6. Les Royales, 7. Les Civiles, 8. Les Historiques, 9. Les Poetiques, 10. Les Magiques, 11. Les Academiques.

39 For a more detailed analysis see Jahn 2005: 82–83, 87–88.

designs used for *Cleopatra* can also be mapped onto these categories.[40] The stage designs, thought of as topoi, are more than mere decoration; they also convey a basic atmosphere and intention. The opera audience can read their iconographic value, and they give priority to the experience rather than historical or geographical accuracy.

Furthermore, the stage design of the baroque opera has to be read in the above-described representational context. The design not only identifies the setting of the action, but also expresses content qualities. It is a telling visual element shaped by the ruler's fame, the grandeur, and the glory, conjuring the magnificence of this figure in the monumentality of the design by giving it extreme architectural dimensions. Any historical truth to facts is at this point out of the question; even something like "antiquity as an imagined space" cannot be found here. The way in which the stage design enhances the plot is thus not by expressing the specific place stated in the libretto. Instead, it is the specific atmosphere and intention identified in the libretto that the stage design strengthens – it thus becomes both atmospheric image (ruin romanticism) and praise of the ruler that is not dependent on ancient sources (palace design). The strategy of visualisation is thus a political one.

II. The scene-painter Pelagio Palagi and his depiction of Egypt in *La morte di Cleopatra* (1797)

How much the function of the stage design is changeable both in a political and in a socio-cultural context is revealed in the depiction of Egypt in the opera *La morte di Cleopatra* (1797). The design of this piece visually communicates with the viewer on a wholly new level, making them the witness of a historical past which is at its core an imagined one.

La morte di Cleopatra is a two-act opera with music by Sebastiano Nasolini, and a libretto by Simeone Antonio Sografi. It was produced on 22 June 1791 at Teatro Eretenio in Vincenza, and it was successful not only in Italy, but also at opera houses of aristocrats across Europe.[41] The Libretto tells a story which ends – as one may guess from the title – with the only possible solution of Cleopatra and Marc Antony dying a death of love. The narrative focuses on their final days, making major changes to the historical course of events. At the very outset, a high priest uses astrological signs to prophesy the doom of Egypt and its Queen Cleopatra. Notwithstanding all strategies of escaping this, fate cannot be stopped. Not long after Marc Antony rides into Alexandria as a victor and lover, the story

40 For example: market square – Les civiles; palace – Les Royales; ruin scene – Les Rustiques; encampment – Les Militaires.

41 For a list of productions see Nocciolini 1994: 330–331.

has Augustus come to the city gates and remind Marc Antonty of his marital obligations towards Augustus' sister Octavia.[42] On behalf of Rome, he demands the political elimination of Marc Antony and termination of Cleopatra's rule. This incites Marc Antony to make an angered challenge. However, the battle is lost and Cleopatra is put in chains. Augustus makes Cleopatra the immoral proposal of sparing Mark Antony on the condition that she be fully his. After initial protest, Cleopatra (seemingly) accepts the deal and thus drives Marc Antony into despair, which leads him to inflict on himself a lethal wound – however he remains alive for the time being. False rumours of his death make Cleopatra feel desolate in her turn, and she seeks to take her own life with a poisonous snake, also to escape the political humiliation of being taken to Rome as a slave. However, Mark Antony, in a state of puzzlement, enters the scene at the last minute. The loving couple finally die under the eyes of their Roman enemies in the darkness of a pyramid, thus expressing their mutual faithfulness.[43]

In 1797, the opera was reproduced at Teatro Comunale di Bologna, with stage design for the final scene in the pyramid created by the artist Pelagio Palagi, who played an important role for the visualisation of historical settings that began in the eighteenth century (figure 5).[44] The design is drawing washed in black ink and showing a semi-circular crypt in a pyramid.

From the crypt, at least two exits lead to column-framed halls. Another exit at the centre suggests a long corridor lying ahead. Where exactly these exits lead is not clear. The stage design features a fascinating repertoire of Egypt-style set pieces: female sphinxes, Egyptian statuettes, hieroglyphs, scarabs, and lions seated on pilasters. Sistra are installed at each side of the doors. The columns are topped with capitals with palmettes and palm leaves. As far for the relevance of this scene to the plot element, i.e. the death of Cleopatra and Marc Antony, this

42 According to historical tradition, Augustus did not reach the city until after winning the battle near Actium, after which Marc Antony had followed Cleopatra on her flight and thus could not possibly have made a victory march into Egypt as he had done after earlier battles.

43 "Für Kleopatra bedeutet der gemeinsame Tod die letzte, ewige Vereinigung, die rückwirkend auch ihrem eigenen Leben einen bislang ungekannten Sinn verleiht. Sie beweist somit ihre constantia, und trägt selbst die Konsequenzen ihrer vorherigen Handlung – dem Treueverrat an Antonius. Die Umgebung der Pyramide stellt dabei den angemessenen Hintergrund für einen solch erhabenen Augenblick dar" (Kost 2006: 177–178); for a detailed analysis of the libretto with changes to the character constellation also see Kost 2006: 257–291.

44 Printed in Humbert et al. 1994, fig 240 with credit to Pelagio Palagi which Jaeger 1997: 266 reiterates in footnote 195. Trezzini, Paganelli (1966: 11), however, reference the artists Braccioli Mauro, Berti Mauro, Luigi Busatti, Clemente Caldesi, Luigi Pranzini and Giuseppe Luccini for the stage design of the 1797 production in their list of librettos at Teatro Comunale di Bologna.

visualisation is at the same time an encoding of the expressed content.[45] It generates an exotic aura pointing to the sublime and the irrational at the same time.[46] The sublime element is created by the crypt in its mere visual reminiscence of death and the thus-arising benign fearfulness, which is typical of the eighteenth-century zeitgeist.

Figure 5: Pelagio Palagi (1775–1818), stage design for *La morte di Cleopatra* by Sebastiano Nasolini, Bologna, 1797: Crypt under a Pyramid (1797); pen and black ink with watercolour on paper; © Biblioteca Comunale dell'Archiginnasio, Gabinetto di Disegni

The irrational aspect stems from the confusion the crypt causes merely by its circular shape, which in itself is not only not Egyptian and thus historically inac-

45 "Als Verehrer der Toten und des Todes wurden die Ägypter schon durch Herodot geschildert. Seitdem galten sie als dasjenige Volk der Antike, bei dem der Totenkult am ausgeprägtesten entwickelt und dessen kulturelles Ziel es gewesen sei, die zerstörerische Macht des Todes durch seine Bauwerke zu überwinden. Gegen Ende des 18. Jahrhunderts glaubte man schließlich sogar in der ägyptischen Landschaft selbst das Totenreich der Griechen gefunden, die elysischen Gefilde, Styx und Lethe wiederentdeckt zu haben" (Syndram 1990: 22).

46 Pulvirenti 2008: 153.

curate, but also connects to the column hall. The coffered ceiling with the second floor is also not architecturally coherent because the pilasters at the bottom have no supporting function and are thus not constructionally plausible. It thus becomes apparent that the stage design is not based on archeological studies – far too disorderly is the spatial arrangement in terms of its architecture. It is a theatrical realisation that generates a mysterious Egyptian atmosphere.

1. The image of Egypt in the 18th century as a basis of reception for the scene painters
There is indeed a wide spectrum of how the Egyptian culture was perceived in the eighteenth century. This is manifest in literary and art treatises, as well as in architecture and the visual arts.

After the publications by Athanius Kircher, another contribution to the image of Egypt was made only in the travel writings by Corneille Le Bruyn[47] in 1698. Le Bruyn's account of his journey through Asia Minor all the way to Egypt and Palestine features a large number of copperplate prints and thus provided an intitial and verifiable insight into the country. This was followed by additional travel writings by Paul Lucas[48] (1719), Frederic Louis Norden[49] (1741) and Richard Pococke[50] (1743). In fact, the books by Norden and Pococke were the most read publications on Egypt. Especially Norden's was unique in its excellent illustrations, and inspired free adoption of Ancient Egypt in all artistic disciplines.[51] Literary works studying antiquity collections were first published in 1719 by Bernard de Montfaucon[52] and in 1752 by Philippe Caylus.[53] Montfaucon's study featuring an extensive print collection of pieces in European collections included all known artifacts and artworks connected to Ancient Egypt, and thanks to its neatly engraved prints became a frequently used source of images for eighteenth century art.[54] In a like manner, Caylus' own antiquity collection provided detailed descriptions of a large number of Egyptian artworks and emphasised

47 Le Bruyn, Corneille: Reizen van Corn. de Bruyn door de vermaardste deelen van Klein Asia, de eylanden Scio, Rhodus, Cyprus enz. mitsg. de voornaamste steden van Aegypten, Syrien en Palestina, Delft 1698; published in 1700 in French and in 1702 in English.

48 Lucas, Paul: Voyage du sieur Paul Lucas fait en 1714 dans la Turquie, l'Asie, la Sourie, la Palestine, la Haute et la Basse-Egypte, Rom 1719.

49 Norden, Frederic Louis: Mémoire sur les ruines de Thèbes en Égypte, London 1741.

50 Pococke, Richard: A description of the East, and some other Countries, London 1743–1745.

51 Pevsner 1968: 195.

52 Montfaucon, Bernard de: Antiquité expliquée et representée en figures, 15 vols., Paris 1719–1724.

53 Caylus, Claude Philippe: Recueil d'antiquités égyptiennes, étrusques, greques, romaines et gauloises, 7 vols, Paris 1752–1767.

54 Syndram 2001: 1199.

their references to eternity.[55] The growing number of publications regarding travel writings and illustrations of Ancient Egypt resonated with the spirit of the time which showed an increased interest in larger constructions of Egyptian antiquity. These were the forerunners of the fashion around Egypt which began in Rome around 1760 and culminated in the publication of Egyptian fireplace designs between 1764 and 1768 and the interior design of Caffè degli Inglesi at Piazza di Spagna in Rome by Giovanni Battista Piranesi.[56]

Pelagio Palagi, aged only 22 in 1797, studied Piranesi's writings in the 1790s and was familiar with the writings and copper prints by Caylus and Montfaucon.[57] His stage design is one of many examples of Egypt-style sketches from the late eighteenth century onwards, including designs for operas, ballets, pantomimes, and musical dramas within the wider Cleopatra theme. Palagi's interest in Egyptian motifs is shown in the abundance of the sketches and copies of Egyptian artifacts in his possession.[58] His design is a manifestation of the change in the aesthetic value of Egyptian art. So far seen only as a preliminary stage of classic Greek art, Egyptian art was now increasingly appreciated[59] and recognised as an art form in its own right.[60] This sentiment was willingly absorbed by artists and turned into colossal designs of Egyptian shapes.[61] This emphasis on the "aesthetic aspect" was a result of the approach taken previously, which had not focused on aesthetics, but on fantasy and was only minutely based on direct observation. Of interest were the many god figures, the Egyptian wisdom, the Egyptian religion, and, especially for opera, the Egyptian anecdotes and tales. It was not, however, the real historical architecture or art, the aesthetics of the sublime, the monumental, and the colossal, and the related ideas of eternity that nourished the budding infatuation with Egypt. Its occult mysteries, their symbolism and light metaphors were incorporated into pseudo-Egyptian rituals whose echo returned in the Age of Enlightenment in associations such as the Free Masons.[62]

---

55 With its references to eternity, it played an important role in the evolution or art described by Caylus as part of an analysis of art of the eighteenth century.

56 Published as a sequence of copper prints in Piranesi, Giovanni Battista, Diverse Maiere d'adornare i cammini etc., Roma 1769.

57 Alvin 1932: 154; Humbert et al. 1994: 397–398.

58 See Jaeger 1997: 206–207, who references 3,000 drawings by Palagi on this subject at Biblioteca dell'Archiginnasio de Bologna; also Roncuzzi 2004: 35–37.

59 Caylus saw Egyptian construction art, along with the Etruscan, as the origin and the basis of all Ancient construction. See Baumgart 1990: 41.

60 Caylus now saw in the Egyptians a wise and enlightened people ("ce peuple sage et éclairé"). For details see Pevsner 1968: 196.

61 Marie-Joseph Peyre; Jean-Louis Desprez; Mauro Tesi.

62 Nocciolini 1994: 333–334; Kost 2006: 162.

2. The conception of history and the function of opera at the end of 18th century

The intermittent one hundred years between the productions of the two Cleopatra-themed operas *Cleopatra* (1690) and *La morte di Cleopatra* (1797) necessarily mean a change in the audience's relationship to the opera. Not only the socio-political conditions, but also the aesthetic expectations and inclinations with regard to opera underwent noticeable changes. Just as the theatre, opera too, ceases to be "a celebration and becomes an instrument of social change".[63] The increased number of *La morte di...* operas after 1790[64] reveals the transition from the baroque *lieto fine*, which was an expression of aristocratic self-esteem, to *tragico fine*, which can be seen in socio-cultural correlation with the progressing evolution of the middle-class society and a new moral analysis of the action. The rights of the individual have to make way for the rights of the large numbers of the middle-class, which also restrains the rights of the absolutist aristocrat with respect to the rights of the large numbers of his subjects. The so-far shining hero of the baroque, as the mirror image of the ruler, must stand up to the trial. In the present example, the opera *La morte di Cleopatra* this means acceptance of death by Cleopatra and Marc Antony, which is tantamount to an admission of fault against Augustus.[65] Sografi, the librettist of the piece, must have been an admirer of writings by Voltaire, which the plot makes visible in the location of the death scene. Cleopatra and Marc Antony die in the gloomy crypt of a pyramid. This Voltaire-esque aesthetics of horror, of suffering, and of tragic can be identified both in Sografi's libretto[66] and in Palagi's artistic realisation in the stage design for the scene.

III. Conclusion

The two presented examples of stage designs for Cleopatra operas are both spatial fantasies of their own time. In both cases, they use enormous and magnificent architectures which, however, oppose each other diametrically, and express the intention of sublimity in different ways.

In the first example, the opera *Cleopatra* from 1690, invocation of grandeur and the power of political sovereignty is achieved with the help of a contemporary palace architecture (act II, acene 8) as well as in the style of common ruin roman-

63 Galle 1991: 16–17.

64 *La morte di Cesare* (1789), *La morte di Semiramide* (1790), *La morte di Cleopatra* (1791), *La morte di Mitridate* (1797); these operas always focused on traditional historical themes, which previously, however, always ended on a heroic-reconsiliatory note. See Hortschansky 1994: 234.

65 Hortschansky 1994: 236–238; whereas Marc Antony accepts death purely for love; on a possible connection between acceptance of death as a theme in the librettos by the Venetian Sografi and the political demise of Venice at the end of the century, also see Hortschansky 1994: 247–248.

66 Dubowy 1979: 844–846; Hortschansky 1994: 243–244.

ticism (act III, acene 1). The stage design becomes a part of a constellation of representations and deferences through which the divine and political power of the ruler is expressed on stage in the obligatory display of magnificence. A historical reference to the actual setting by way of ancient visual set pieces is not required. Despite the availability of a basis of visual adoption of Ancient Egypt, there is no need to depict Alexandria through Egypt-style shapes. The historical dimension is made clear by the typological linkages. The local iconography of the ruler in the contemporary architecture is sufficient to establish a connection to the royal court of the pharaos in Alexandria. The content of the opera and the characterisations of its protagonists are in close correlation with the occasion of its production – it is a visual and vocal glorification of the ruler.

This is quite different in the case of *La morte di Cleopatra* from 1797. The *tragico fine* in the meantime is a familiar sight on eighteenth-century stages. Aside from these generic conventions with regard to the subject matter, the political conditions of the opera have changed, allowing new space for interpretive freedom. Palagi had demonstrably been exposed to ancient Egyptian shapes and plays with the mythical and mysterious aura that surrounds Egypt. In doing so, this adoption of antiquity does not seek to express any ancient Egyptian reality. The Egyptian-style set pieces are rather interpreted and combined to build an impression that generally seems Egyptian.[67] The quality of ancient Egyptian architecture of referencing the eternal, on the one hand, attests to aesthetic sublimity merely by dint of its monumentality. On the other hand, it is symbolic of the action described in the libretto through the sublimity of its message.

In both cases, the architecture represented in the stage design is a telling kind of architecture which expresses its 'venerable' status through different motifs. The particular iconography of the architecture changes because of an altered aesthetic approach to architecture and its political interpretations. It is not until the end of the eighteenth century that Egyptian architecture becomes worthy of depiction – both in stage design and in the architectural theory of the time. For the present essay, it is of interest to note that the adoption of ancient Egyptian constructional elements is at bottom not in correlation with the depiction of a figure of Egyptian history such as Cleopatra. Well into the eighteenth century, showing a historically accurate setting is of no relevance for the visualisation of an opera with an Egyptian theme. The visual transition in the stage design of the opera first occurs towards the end of the eighteenth century and is a result of aesthetic and sociocultural factors.

67 "Sie gestalten ihr Sujet auf ägyptische Weise, 'á l'egyptienne'" (Fitzenreiter 2007: 326–327); intentions of historical accuracy are not yet to be found. This ambition will change in the nineteenth century.

At that time, operas featuring the figure of Cleopatra, once again, experienced an enormous increase in popularity. The cause of this was Napoleon's campaign to Egypt, which triggered an outright Egypt-mania. As a result, more space was given, again, to exoticising depictions of Cleopatra, most importantly including a lascivious kind of femininity.[68] Furthermore, the special role played by Egyptian religiosity (cult of Isis), which had already been given quite some space in *La morte di Cleopatra*, made the imagination of Egypt on the opera stage even more colourful.

Bibliography

Alvin 1932 = F. Alvin, s.v. Palagi Pelagio, in: Lexikon der bildenden Künstler von der Antike bis zur Gegenwart, vol. 26, Leipzig 1932, 154–155.

Baumgart 1990 = F. Baumgart, Ägyptische und klassizistische Baukunst. Ein Beitrag zu den Wandlungen architektonischen Denkens in Europa, in: K. Philipp (ed.), Revolutionsarchitektur. Klassische Beiträge zu einer unklassischen Architektur, Braunschweig 1990, 34–55.

Curran 2009 = B. Curran, Obelisk. A History, Cambridge 2009.

Degen 1935 = H. Degen, Friedrich Christian Bressand. Ein Beitrag zur Braunschweig-Wolfenbüttler Theatergeschichte, Braunschweig 1935.

Dubowy 1979 = N. Dubowy, s.v. Sografi, in: Die Musik in Geschichte und Gegenwart. Allgemeine Enzyklopädie der Musik, Suppl. 16, Kassel 1979, 844–845.

Eisinger 1990 = R. Eisinger, Braunschweiger Werkstücke. Das Hagenmarkt-Theater in Braunschweig (1690–1861), Braunschweig 1990.

Feichtinger 1996 = B. Feichtinger, Die eine und die vielen. Identität und Variation im literarischen Kleopatra-Bild von der Antike bis zu Shakespeare, Literaturwissenschaftliches Jahrbuch 37 (1996), 89–112.

Frenzel 2005 = E. Frenzel, s.v. Kleopatra, in: E. Frenzel (ed.), Stoffe der Weltliteratur. Ein Lexikon dichtungsgeschichtlicher Längsschnitte, Stuttgart [10]2005, 509–514.

Fitzenreiter 2007 = M. Fitzenreiter, Europäische Konstruktionen Altägyptens. Der Fall Ägyptologie, in: T. Glück – L. Morenz (eds.), Exotisch, Weisheitlich und Uralt. Europäische Konstruktionen Altägyptens, Hamburg 2007, 323–350.

Galle 1991 = R. Galle, Über den Helden im Drama des 17. und 18. Jahrhunderts, in: K. Hortschansky (ed.), Opernheld und Opernheldin im 18. Jahrhundert. Aspekte der Librettoforschung. Ein Tagungsbericht, Hamburg – Eisenach 1991, 9–20.

Hofstetter 2005 = E. Hofstetter, Wiederentdeckung Ägyptens in Europa. Reiseberichte als Informationsquelle zu ägyptischer Kunst, in: M. Kunze – E. Hofstetter (eds.), Die Wiederentdeckung der ägyptischen Kunst im 18. Jahrhundert. Winckelmann und Ägypten (Ausst.-Kat. Winckelmann-Museum Stendal und Staatliches Museum Ägyptischer Kunst München), Stendal 2005, 9–20.

Hortschansky 1991 = K. Hortschansky, Der tragische Held in der italienischen Oper am Ende des 18. Jahrhunderts, in: K. Hortschansky (ed.), Opernheld und Opernheldin im 18. Jahrhundert. Aspekte der Librettoforschung. Ein Tagungsbericht, Hamburg – Eisenach 1991, 233–252.

68 For example: Thèophile Gautier, Une nuit de Clèopatre, 1838.

Humbert et al. 1994 = J.-M. Humbert – M. Pantazzi – C. Ziegler, Egyptomania. Egypt in Western Art 1730–1930, Ausst. Kat. Musée du Louvre, Paris 1994, National Gallery of Canada, Ottawa 1994, Kunsthistorisches Museum, Wien 1994–1995, Chicago 1994.

Jaeger 1997 = B. Jaeger, Giuseppe Jappelli, le Café Pedrocchi de Padoue et la redécouverte de L'Egypte en Italie, in: E. Staehelin – Jaeger, Bertrand (eds.), Ägypten-Bilder. Akten des Symposions zur Ägypten-Rezeption, Augst bei Basel vom 9.–11. September 1933, Göttingen 1997 (Orbis Biblicus et Orientalis 150), 187–299.

Jahn 2005 = B. Jahn, Die Sinne und die Oper. Sinnlichkeit und das Problem ihrer Versprachlichung im Musiktheater des nord- und mitteldeutschen Raumes (1680–1740), Tübingen 2005.

Kost 2006 = K. Kost, Das *tragico fine* auf venezianischen Opernbühnen des späten 18. Jahrhunderts, Diss. Heidelberg 2006, http://archiv.ub.uni-heidelberg.de/volltextserver/6611/ (last accessed October 2016).

Leospo 1989 = E. Leospo, Athanasius Kircher und das Museo Kircheriano, in: G. Sievernich – H. Budde (eds.), Europa und der Orient. 800–1900 (Ausst.-Kat. 4. Festival der Weltkulturen Horizonte Berlin 1989), Gütersloh – München 1989, 56–71.

Marquardt 2013 = J. Marquardt, s.v. Kleopatra, in: DNP Suppl 8, Stuttgart 2013, 551–576.

Nocciolini 1994 = M. Nocciolini, Circolazione di un melodramma e rivolgimenti politici (1796–1799). La morte di Cleopatra, Studi musicali 13/2 (1994), 329–365.

Pevsner 1968 = N. Pevsner, Architektur und Design. Von der Romantik zur Sachlichkeit, München 1968.

Pulvirenti 2008 = G. Pulvirenti, Ägyptenrezeption im 18. Jahrhundert, in: V. Rosenberger (ed.), "Die Ideale der Alten". Antikenrezeption um 1800, Stuttgart 2008 (Friedenstein-Forschungen 3), 153–165.

Reischert 2001 = A. Reischert, s.v. Kleopatra, in: Kompendium der musikalischen Sujets. Ein Werkkatalog, vol. 1, Kassel 2001, 587–584.

Richter 1963 = H. Richter, Johann Oswald Harms. Ein deutscher Theaterdekorateur des Barock, Emsdetten, Westfalen 1963.

Roncuzzi Roversi Monaco 2004 = V. Roncuzzi Roversi Monaco, Pelagio Palagi all'Archiginnasio, in: C. Bernardini (ed.), Pelagio Palagi alle Collezioni Comunali d'Arte, Bologna 2004, 35–37.

Rosand 1991 = E. Rosand, Opera in Seventeenth-Century Venice. The Creaton of a Genre, Berkeley – Los Angeles – Oxford 1991.

Schröder 1998 = D. Schröder, Zeitgeschichte auf der Opernbühne. Barockes Musiktheater in Hamburg im Dienst von Politik und Diplomatie (1690–1745), Göttingen 1998 (Abhandlungen zur Musikgeschichte 2).

Seebald 2009 = C. Seebald, Libretti vom "Mittelalter". Entdeckungen von Historie in der (nord)deutschen und europäischen Oper um 1700, Tübingen 2009.

Siegmund 2002 = A. Siegmund, Die romantische Ruine im Landschaftsgarten. Ein Beitrag zum Verhältnis der Romantik zu Barock und Klassik, Würzburg 2002.

Simonis 2004 = A. Simonis, Theatralität und mythologische Repräsentation. Zur Mythologisierung von Geschichte in den europäischen Kleopatra-Dramen der frühen Neuzeit, in: A. Simonis – L. Simonis (eds.), Mythen in Kunst und Literatur. Tradition und kulturelle Repräsentation, Köln 2004, 273–292.

Stadt Braunschweig 1990 = Stadt Braunschweig (ed.), 300 Jahre Theater in Braunschweig 1690–1990 (Ausst. Kat. Herzog Anton Ulrich-Museum), Braunschweig 1990.

Stieger 1975 = F. Stieger, s.v. Cleopatra, in: Opernlexikon. Titelkatalog, vol. 1, Tutzing 1975, 252.

zu Stolberg-Wernigerode 1966 = O. zu Stolberg-Wernigerode, s.v. Harm(e)s, in: Neue Deutsche Biografie, vol. 1, Berlin 1966, 684–685.

Syndram 1990 = D. Syndram, Ägypten-Faszinationen. Untersuchungen zum Ägyptenbild im europäischen Klassizismus bis 1800, Frankfurt am Main 1990 (Europäische Hochschulschriften 28, Kunstgeschichte 104).

Syndram 2001 = D. Syndram, s.v. Orient-Rezeption, in: DNP 15/1, Stuttgart 2001, 1194–1210.

Tintelnot 1939 = H. Tintelnot, Barocktheater und barocke Kunst. Die Entwicklungsgeschichte der Fest- und Theater-Dekoration in ihrem Verhältnis zur barocken Kunst, Berlin 1939.

Trezzini – Paganelli 1966 = L. Trezzini – S. Paganelli (eds.), Due secoli di vita musicale. Storia del Teatro Comunale di Bologna, vol. 2, Repertorio critico degli spettacoli e delle esecuzioni musicali dal 1763 al 1966, Bologna 1966.

Vosskamp 1967 = W. Vosskamp, Zeit- und Geschichtsauffassung im 17. Jahrhundert bei Gryphius und Lohenstein, Bonn 1967.

Werr 2010 = S. Werr, Politik mit sinnlichen Mitteln. Oper und Fest am Münchner Hof (1680–1745), Köln – Weimar – Wien 2010.

List of Contributors

Kerstin Droß-Krüpe is currently employed as a post-doctoral assistant at Kassel University. She studied Classical Archaeology, Ancient History and Business Administration at Philipps-Universität Marburg and obtained her PhD in 2010 with a thesis concerning textile production during the Roman Empire in the province of Egypt, which was published as *Wolle – Weber – Wirtschaft. Die Textilproduktion der römischen Kaiserzeit im Spiegel der papyrologischen Überlieferung* (Wiesbaden 2011). In 2014 and 2016 she (co-)edited several volumes on ancient economic history: *Textile Trade and Distribution in Antiquity* (Wiesbaden 2014), *Textiles, Trade, and Theories* (Münster 2016, with Marie-Louise Nosch), *The Cultural Shaping of the Ancient Economy* (Wiesbaden 2016, with Sabine Föllinger and Kai Ruffing). In addition to ancient economic history and ancient textile studies, her research focuses on the reception of antiquity. Her current research project deals with the reception of the 'Babylonian' queen Semiramis in Baroque opera.

Agnès Garcia-Ventura is "Juan de la Cierva" post-doctoral fellow at the IPOA, Universitat de Barcelona. She was awarded her PhD by the Universitat Pompeu Fabra (Barcelona, Spain) in 2012 with a thesis on the textile production in Ur III Mesopotamia. Before her current position, she was a "Material Text Cultures Research Fellow" at the Collaborative Research Centre 933, "Material Texts Cultures", of the Ruprecht-Karls-Universität in Heidelberg (November 2012–May 2013) and she was "Beatriu de Pinós" post-doctoral fellow at the Sapienza, Università di Roma, from October 2014 to September 2016. She also worked for one academic year as Assistant Professor at the Universitat Autònoma de Barcelona (2013–2014). Her main areas of interest are gender studies (especially their application to Assyriology), historiography of Ancient Near Eastern studies, the organization of work in Mesopotamia and ancient musical performance (in both Mesopotamia and the Phoenician and Punic contexts).

Valeska Hartmann is a doctoral candidate at the department of Art History at Philipps-Universität Marburg. Her research project deals with the reception of Antiquity and Orientalism in the stage design of the *opera seria* of the 18th and 19th century. In addition to that her main areas of interest are the history of science, late antique and early Christian art, as well as ancient and medieval sculpture.

Marta Ortega Balanza is a researcher in the group "Tàcita Muta, Grup d'Estudis de Dones i Gènere" (Group of Studies on Women and Gender). She graduated in Law and in History at the Universidat de Barcelona, and postgraduated in

Oriental Studies at the Universitat Pompeu Fabra (Barcelona, Spain). Her publications and lectures focus on women in the ancient history and gender relationships in ancient world, from the view of law and legal sources.

Kerstin Weiand is currently holding the position of an assistant professor at the department of Early Modern History at Philipps-Universität Marburg. After studying history and classical philology in Marburg and Florence, she worked as a lecturer in various positions at the universities in Marburg and Gießen and at the "Società Internazionale per lo studio del medievo latino" in Florence. From 2013 to 2016 she held the position of a post-doctoral fellow at the cluster of excellence "Normative Orders" at the Goethe University Frankfurt. In 2012, she completed her doctoral thesis with a study on the memory of Queen Elizabeth I and political communication in Early Stuart England, which was published as *Herrscherbilder und politische Normbildung. Die Darstellung Elisabeths I. im England des 17. Jahrhunderts* (Göttingen 2015). Furthermore, she published a monograph on the policy of the imperial estates during the Thirties' Years War: *Hessen-Kassel und die Reichsverfassung* (Marburg 2009). She currently works on a project, which examines the idea of the crusade in Early Modern papal politics.